KU-253-292

DUMONT'S LEXICON OF
WINE

Christina Fischer

Photographs by
Armin Faber
and
Thomas Pothmann

All information in this book has been provided to the best knowledge of the author and has been tested by her as well as the publishers with the greatest possible care. It can nevertheless not be assumed that all mistakes are completely excluded. By supplying this information, the author does not assume any responsibility nor does the author provide any form of guarantee. Neither party is responsible for any possible incorrect information supplied in the text.

© 2004 Rebo International b.v., Lisse, The Netherlands

This 2nd edition reprinted in 2006.

Draft: Christina Fischer, Ingo Swoboda
Text and editing: Christina Fischer, Ingo Swoboda in cooperation with Astrid Müllers
Photographs: Armin Faber, Thomas Pothmann
Typesetting: AdAm Studio, Prague, The Czech Republic
Cover design: AdAm Studio, Prague, The Czech Republic

Translation: Janusz Karpeta for Agentura Abandon, Prague, The Czech Republic
Proofreading: Emily Sands, Eva Munk

ISBN 13: 978-90-366-1694-2
ISBN 10: 90-366-1694-8

All rights reserved. No part of this publication may be reproduced, stored in a retrieval system, or transmitted in any form or by any means, electronic, mechanical, photocopying, recording or otherwise, without the prior written permission of the copyright holder.

Contents

Introduction

How does one become a wine expert? The question has become especially pertinent recently, as the world of wines is becoming more complicated and the constantly growing number of varieties does not make appreciation much easier. It is no longer possible to have a mere passing understanding of wine.

The best foundation for a true knowledge of wines includes familiarity with the functions of the senses, with the world of wine flavors and with the various cultivation areas and their types of wine.

Appreciation of wine requires sound rudimentary knowledge. Someone with a taste for wine finds it an exciting topic, well worth investigating and exploring further. And exploring the world of wine will not only please your mouth, but will also let your soul wander freely: wine consumption is a good way to relax from daily stress.

I hope you will find this book both pleasurable and instructive.

Yours, Christina Fischer

WINE FASCINATION

Why wine? Wine has always taken a special place among alcoholic beverages, whether as an everyday drink or as a luxury product. No other drink has left such a lasting mark, changed landscapes, cultures, poetry and literature in the course of the mankind's history, as much as wine. The large winemaking areas in the world are witness to a constantly changing wine culture. With the spread of consumption in the grapegrowing regions, each regional cuisine developed its own dynamics in order to find a balance between good food and drink. Wine is a living product, intense and sometimes exuberant. Its variety and range of flavors and tastes make it a unique article of consumption and an indication of mankind's sophistication.

Each bottle of wine is marked by its origin, taste balance and, most importantly, by the winegrower: these are "fingerprints" for connoisseurs.

Rendezvous of the senses

Rendezvous of the senses

Taking pleasure in the senses? Yes, but not all senses are as complicated and complex as the sense of taste. We can swiftly and precisely ascertain whether wine is cold or warm. However, the taste and composition of wine renders most people speechless. You thought it was simple: you like drinking wine, you have your favorites and you know how to value a good drop at a party. However, when some colleagues or friends really get going, they leave you cold. Terms like "beguiling nose," "typical flavors," and "bad aftertaste" loom large – incomprehensible vocabulary obscure great thoughts. On the other hand, you cannot define the various flavors and smells, nor describe how they really smell and taste. Don't panic, that is normal. Wine tasting is actually not difficult; everyone knows the common flavors, smells and tastes found in wines. Our taste buds exist from birth. We encounter var-

ious flavors in varying degrees of intensity. From the beginning of our life, all perceived smells are stored in our memory. In order to be able to recall smells and flavors in our mind, some patience is needed. Practice makes perfect. That also means tasting, tasting and once again tasting. As you would expect, it must be done in moderation and with common sense. Drunkenness never sharpened anyone's perceptions and delicate nuances will pass you by if you succumb to the toxic power of wine.

Over time, constantly gaining new flavor impressions and experiences, you will come to understand and learn to define, with the greatest of ease, the differences. Wine is, therefore, not so complicated, but it shows its variety in many shades. No other drink has such a complex combination of favors and is composed of so many elements as wine. Not all the components of wine can be immediately discovered or tasted. Some are hidden and subtle and can only be recognized with time and practice. Others are volatile and dramatic and will strike the novice taster right away. Wine is exciting. The first step is the recognition of flavors through the senses.

SENSE AS AN INSTRUMENT

Our senses are a window onto the world; they help us define and categorize various impressions in their proper place. They restrict our world and determine what is recognizable. Although the senses can be affected, dulled even, by moods and feelings, we can only ascertain as much from the environment as the senses can convey.

In tasting a wine, the taster must rely entirely on his senses. At first glance, seeing, smelling and tasting appear relatively simple steps in assessing a wine. Yet only a few people are aware of the possibilities and limits of the senses. An understanding of their functions can be helpful in order to comprehend and organize certain perceptions, to train them systematically, and to make optimal use of these experiences.

THE EYE DRINKS AS WELL

The first impression is always an optical one. Not much escapes the eye. It is said that the eye eats. In our case, it drinks. Take a look at the wine, but do not be misled. Because man lives primarily in a world of vision, there is a great possibility of blurred perception and deceptive reality. The eye cannot itself assess any wine, or even say with 100% certainty that there is wine in the glass! In certain cases, apple juice can have a color similar to a mature wine. The eye is not capable of making a clear distinction between the flavor differences.

The eye test must first analyze the color, shade and clearness of the wine. To analyze the color of the wine, always raise the glass by the stem – so that it stays clean and transparent – a little bit diagonally opposite the light or against a white background. The wine has to be completely clear in the light and the surface of the wine should be perfectly pure. White wines must be pure and completely transparent, although older white wines are sometimes amber-colored.

Small, mostly transparent crystals, the so-called tartar, are natural substances and do not affect the quality of the wine. Sometimes the wine shows cloudiness or fine separated floating articles and flakes, but such lumps of unwanted substances do not necessarily affect the wine quality negatively. In red wines, such cloudiness always appears and usually consists of completely harmless tannin and artificial coloring. In particular, old vintages contain powdery grounds of eliminated artificial coloring and tannin, which get stirred up when slightly shaken. For that reason, before opening old wines, one should allow them a quiet period so that the deposit at the bottom of the bottle can settle. Some wines

TIP

For a better optical assessment of a wine, place the wine glass against a white background. Then, you will see through dark red wine.

leave heavy drops, known as church windows, on the glass after you tip the glass. This phenomenon is a reliable indication of the abundance of the extract. The more refined the "window," the higher the glycerin content in the wine. Glycerin, a by-product of alcoholic fermentation, is a non-toxic, syrup-like, thick alcohol and is ranked among the most important substances in the wine, giving it its full-bodied flavor and character.

ALWAYS TRUST THE NOSE

There is nothing more noticeable on a face than the nose. It is logical, since, until now, no scientific or technical apparatus has surpassed the sensitivity and efficiency of the human nose. Moreover, smells and fragrances leave an intense, and often involuntary, mark in our memory. Our sense of smell is unerring, but also very individual. A smell that some people find especially obtrusive is sometimes not even noticed by other people in the room. No other sense affects the mood and emotions as much as smell. Good smells arouse nice memories. It is therefore not surprising that the sense of smell for an adult often evokes powerful childhood memories.

A healthy person can differentiate between about 4000 smells.

Man can sense danger with his nose: scent molecules can indicate fire, putrid water or acrid scents. Thus nature has arranged that man cannot avoid smells. You can do without other sense impressions: you can close or cover your eyes or avoid physical contact, but the sense of smell is relentless. Tiny scent molecules are transmitted with every breath to the sensitive scent cells of the mucosa. However, the sense of smell is imperfect and only strong smells reach the mucosa and brings about perception.

Taste would not be possible without smell because the wide range of the smells found in the wine are first transmitted transparently and perceptibly through the sense of smell. When biting or swallowing, you can also smell with the palate. Fine and delicate aromas found in wine must be purposefully transported to the right place in the nose. Through sniffing, man creates small air swirls which drive the various scent substances to the mucosa situated in the protected upper part of the nose. Even the finest and most volatile smells are often recognizable by the non-trained nose: lemon, mint, coffee, tobacco, rose aromas, and many others.

The next step is the emotional reaction. By shaking the glass, a mix of ethereal oils and scent substances are developed in an air swirl and driven to the mucosa. Bad smells like a strong sulfuric stink, a putrescent stench (the smell of bad eggs) or a vinegary smell is easily recognizable. The person who has emptied the glass should put his nose inside again, in order to breathe the scent substances left on the glass. Any perceived aromas originate from the tannin and the wood of its cask.

ANYTHING FOR FLAVOR

They say that someone who can smell well also has a good sense of taste. Proper taste is affected by the perception on the mucosa. These perceptions, which have already been gained by the eye and nose, often prove true on the palate. Moreover, new perceptions arise through the warming up of the wine on the palate. In comparison with the variety and intensity of aromas perceived by the mucosa, the tongue acts as a rough sense instrument. Since the taste buds on the tongue respond to sweetness, sharpness, bitterness and saltiness, you should put enough wine on your palate that to distribute the liquid over the entire surface of the tongue. In order to have the most intense taste perception possible, you must roll the wine over the tongue regularly back and forth. Audible slurping and chewing of the wine while sucking the air is allowed in wine tasting. In restaurants, it is advisable to avoid this auditory experience. At the moment of swallowing, the perception is the most powerful. In the area of the tongue roots, where the scent papillae are located, the perceptions linger longer than in the front part of the tongue. When someone refers to a bad aftertaste, he means that a strong smell perception lingers on in the rear part of the tongue area.

When tasting, it is recommended to keep the wine on the palate for about ten seconds and to swallow a small portion once or twice. During the first assessment, the wine is perceived as dry or sweet. But be careful! Sweet aromas are predominant and it is advisable to wait before assessing too quickly! Furthermore, the real sugar content is easily underestimated when the sharpness content is high. As a result, it is a common mistake to claim that a dry wine is a sharp wine. A dry wine does not contain more sharpness, it only seems sharper because it is not as sweet as other wines. An unpleasant, biting sharpness indicates the immaturity of the grapes during the harvest. In the case of red wines, tannin, which comes from the grape stems, seeds from the wood of the cask, makes up the structure of the wine. Sophisticated red wines from warm climates are often rough and non-harmonic due to the predominant tannin in their youth, but they become fine and velvety as they age.

TEST: BOUNDARIES OF TASTE

Precise taste can be trained. You just need:

Sugar (icing sugar is particularly soluble), common salt, a bit of caffeine, and for each substance, one quart of tasteless, still water.

Weigh out 0.007 oz of each substance on a quart digital scale on a sheet of greaseproof paper, and put this quantity in a quart of water. (There should be one quart of water for each substance.)

Stir well and taste. Let the taste sample act on the tongue for a while. Do you recognize a taste?

Then, for each sample, add 0.007 oz of each substance sequentially and note when you can classify clearly the taste as sweet, salty or bitter.

Usually, the perception bounds are: between 0.017 and 0.141 oz per quart for sugar, between 0.0035 and 0.0352 oz per quart for common salt and 0.0035 to 0.007 oz per quart for caffeine.

A brief history of wine cultivation

A brief history of wine cultivation

History is a crucial part of wine cultivation. A great deal can be deduced from the past and, if you want to understand wine, it makes sense to know something about its origin. Still, through the centuries, little has been known or understood about winemaking.

For a long time, wine has been an indispensable part of each meal. In many diverse cultures, it reigns supreme as an everyday drink and it is a symbol of good health and status in richer countries.

The systematic development of winemaking, or wine culture, is inseparably connected with the origin of European civilization. Winemaking first emerged in the pharaohs' Egypt in about 4000 BC. Traveling along the trade routes, wine reached the most important trading centers in the Mediterranean. In Greece, winemaking quickly became a lucrative and successful economic endeavor. As early as the second half of the second century before Christ, there were areas of grape cultivation throughout Greece and on the Aegean Islands. Greek settlers brought grapevines to the southern Italy, France and Sicily at the beginning of the first century.

In the 17th century, the current and familiar wine bottle came into being. Till then, wine was transported and stored in amphora and casks. It was served directly from the cask into the cup.

With the rise of Rome as a world power, the grapevine also reached the colder

northern areas of central Europe. Under Roman rule, centers of the European wine culture emerged from Wachau all the way to Bordeaux and Rioja. After the disintegration of the Roman Empire, European wine production stagnated. Only the monasteries continued the Roman wine culture, developing new and innovative cultivation and processing methods. The power of wine as a symbol of Christ's blood, its vital place in the holy mass and its solid economic value as a popular commodity motivated the monasteries to encourage the spread of vineyards across all of Europe. The Cistercians and Benedictines in particular experimented with soils, conditions and types of wine and laid the foundations for "wine knowledge," as it is currently understood.

In the middle of the 16th century, the first vineyards were developed in the area in South America today known as Chile. Wine had already become absolutely vital to everyday life in Europe. As a drink, it was healthier than water because of the resistance of alcohol to bacteria and filth. The relatively long durability of wine allowed people to build up supplies during crisis periods. During sieges, wine was as necessary to the survival of the besieged city as the food supply. Wine was on board every ship, including those that intrepid circumnavigators and explorers of the 15th and 16th centuries brought to America for the first time. It was these early explorers who brought European grape vines to the American continent.

A disease called Phylloxera almost brought European winemaking to a standstill in the middle of the 19th century. In 1880, the imported graft grapevines – European grapevines based on American models – proved to be immune to the disease and guaranteed the continuity of many European winegrowing areas.

In the 20th century, the cultivated winemaking areas and production quantities declined continually. However, additional overseas winemaking areas were established. Towards the turn of the millennium, winemaking areas amounted to about 20 million acres.

The Romans used corks for closing wine vessels. However, it was not until the 17th century that the cork, as a stopper, became commonly used.

How does wine come into being?

How does wine come into being?

Good wines start in the vineyards.

What exactly is wine? The German Wine Act gives the following definition: "wine is a product that is gained exclusively through the complete and partially alcoholic fermentation of fresh, mixed grapes or grape must."

Wines are not "made" then, at least not in cellars anyway! Wines come from grape must and that requires grapes as a starting material.

Consequently, the type of wine, the soil conditions and the individual processing by the winegrower are fundamental to making a good wine. Besides, there is always a risk of changing climatic circumstances, which present a challenge for each vintage, along with the risk of bad crops.

Grapes

Wines are made from grapes cultivated with the art and knowledge of the winegrower. Selection of the grapevine is a decisive factor in the aroma and taste of the wine. Not all grapevines thrive in every world location, although the grapevine is generally regarded as a tough and adaptable plant. Some grapes like hot climates and others prefer chilly weather. However, in the long history of winemaking, by means of new cultivation or clones, certain grapevines have been adapted to specific environments. Worldwide, most wines are made using grapes from various grapevines, the so-called Cuvées. Since the grapevine itself, in various concentrations and portions, forms the character of the wine, the winegrower can respond considerably better to the possible vintage variations and different grades of maturity of the grapes by using multiple vines rather than by sticking to so-called "pure" wine from one type of the grapevine.

The grapevine is the greatest sugar collector among fruit plants in the world. It can build sugar in the form of fructose and glucose and store it in its grapes.

SOIL

Each acre, each field and every vineyard has a vegetation history. Tested over the centuries, empirical values form the foundation of winemaking because each type of grapevine prefers a specific set of soil conditions.

The composition of the soil, whether slate, gravel, sand or clay, is reflected in both the character and natural climate. In particular, mineral clay is the most prominent and thus determines the fullness of the wine.

Terroir

It is not only the soil that is accountable for the quality and character of the wine. Soil is a composition of various factors, which, summarized briefly, can be referred to as terroir. Terroir is crucial to wine because it represents the natural totality of the soil structure, soil disposition, climates and the cultural and historical heritage of the grapevine or vineyard itself. The connected typification and the conditioned traditions of winegrowing are called terroir. The winegrower's job is to create harmony among the particular conditions.

Climate

One of the most important features, which directly affects the vegetation and the maturity grade of the grapevine, is the climate. As with other fruits, the grapes require a certain amount of sun to reach optimal maturity. Grapes such as Riesling prefer cooler growing areas; others – Zinfandel for instance – require a warm climate to grow properly. American scientists proceed on the assumption that a wine cultivation area has to show at least 2500 sunny hours during the year and an average temperature of 50°F. In Germany, for example, 1600 sunny hours

per year are enough to make grape cultivation possible.

Winegrowing takes place between the 51st and 36th degree of latitude.

If the climatic conditions in one region vary and show uneven values, the region is said to have a microclimate. These smallest climatic units can explain why certain types of vines are optimal in particular locations. Reasons for climatic peculiarities can be found in the so-called sliding slopes, particularly in the accumulated soil structures and their water absorption capabilities.

All these features form the basis for a healthy and mature vintage, from which the quality of the wine results.

Wine production begins in the vineyard. The agreement of the vine type with the soil, climate and location is one of the most important aspects of winemaking. The vines require constant, careful treatment and care. Herbicides and pesticides are applied only in rare cases. From the first breaking out of the vine buds to the full maturity of the vines in the fall, the vine undergoes countless vegetation phases. Blossoming periods in Europe are defined according to the region, usually taking place between mid-May and mid-June. At the beginning of October, the vintage begins in most German wine cultivation areas. The top companies generally harvest the grapes manually, hand-picking only the mature and healthy vines.

How does wine become colored?

Freshly squeezed grapes normally have a gray-green color, no matter if the grapes are white or red. A special procedure is necessary to achieve the color of the wine in the production of red wine. The grape skins, which vary according to the type of the vine, contain substances – with the exception of sugar – which determine the quality of the wine. Apart from tannin and parts of taste substances, there are also color pigments, such as anthocyane, which are soluble in alcohol. The more mature the grape, the higher the color pigment concentration, which explains why red wines from the south have a considerably stronger red color than those grown in the northern wine cultivation regions. If the grape skins are torn slightly during the pressing or grinding processes, the must comes into contact with the opened grape skins and draws its color. For the production of rosé wines, a couple of hours are enough to give a rose-color to the must.

On the other hand, if the red wine grapes are pressed quickly, without a long period of fermentation, then hardly any color pigments reach the must and the must is white.

Into the bottle

When we say "wine preparation," we mean preparation of the grapes for wine. The condition of the grapes is the most decisive factor in the quality of the wine because a good wine can only come from good and healthy grapes. Despite the increasing mechanization of the fieldwork, quality-oriented winegrowing estates are again focusing on the use of more expensive manual labor. Precision, sensibility and individually adapted work are preferable to the faster and more convenient machine processing because the quality of handpicked grapes is superior. Harvesters who do not distinguish between healthy and bad grapes are not used by top winegrowing estates.

On the other hand, cellar technique, which guarantees a certain hygiene standard, is mechanized. Fermenting generally takes place in the computer-controlled cold of the stainless steel cask. The pressing of the grapes and the pumping of the must, as well as the filtrating of the young wine and the filling of the wine are managed almost exclusively mechanically. Prior to the development of the stainless steel casks, all wines were aged in wooden casks. The modern "cask wines" lack the taste typical of the wines grown in traditional wooden casks.

It is often the case that red and white wines are aged in smaller casks (225 quart), called Barriques. The oak wood has a particular impact on the wine. In the Barrique wines, one can usually perceive hints of vanilla, wood and other roasted aromas. The fermenting of wines in stainless steel casks is, however, considerably cheaper than fermenting wine in Barriques. The small casks can only be used a few times because the de-

sired wood taste is gradually lost with each usage. Many wine cultivators use them only once.

White wine

There are many steps before must fills the bottle as finished wine. The process begins in the fall. Right after the vintage, the grapes are transported to the winepress hall so that they can be processed further within a short period of time. The process begins by pressing, two methods of which are commonly used. Some winegrowers let their grapes run through a machine which stems the grapes. With the method of pressing whole stems, necessary for the production of champagne, the grapes are pressed with the stems together. This procedure is much gentler, for the grape skin bursts only during the pressing procedure. According to the type of vine, the grade of maturity and the health conditions of the grapes, the pressure of the pressing is measured and controlled.

As soon as the must is pressed, it is poured into the fermentative vessels. At this moment, yeast starts its job and converts fructose into alcohol. Pure cultivated yeast is added if there is not enough yeast in the must, so that the fermentation can be started. Pure cultivated yeast – as opposed to wild yeast – is predictable and reduces the risk of the must being badly fermented. If the fermentation process is successful, the wine will not take on any unpleasant aftertastes. White wines take between three to five weeks to ferment. Fine, sweet wines take three

months. The pace of fermentation depends on the temperature in the cellar or in the fermentative vessel: the higher the temperature, the faster the fermentation.

Controlled cooling very often influences the fermentation process. Lower temperatures make yeast sluggish and lead to slowed fermentation. Thus, fine aromas are obtained particularly in the case of white wines. Wines for quick consumption are usually piquant and the taste is distinctly fruity. When the fermentation has finished, the young wine is pumped into storage tanks where the maturing process of the young wine begins. The wine is then filtered and poured into bottles.

Red wine

Grinding and stem removing are classic procedures for red wine production. The so-called must is created from a pulp of must and grape skins, which ferment in open stainless steel casks or in wooden must casks. Red wines usually ferment faster than white wines. Due to oxygen contact, yeast reproduces quicker in open casks than in the closed vessels and the fermentation process is faster. Concurrently, in the course of alcoholic fermentation, the extraction of color and tannin substances from the grape skins takes place, giving a red color to the white grape juice. Color substances are dissolved by alcohol created by the transformation of sugar during the fermentative process.

The extraction is additionally supported by the warmth which arises during the fermentation in the must. The red color pigments are extracted, which takes longer with tannin. How long red wine remains in the must depends on the fermentation temperature. The lower the temperature, the longer the must ferments. Nowadays, the temperature of almost all red wines is controlled and managed by cooling systems. Simple wines usually remain in the must for scarcely one week. High quality red wines can be left in the must for up to four weeks. In smaller vintage years, when the skins and tannin contain little color, the wines remain in the must only a relatively short time.

Following the alcoholic fermentation, all red wines go through a second fermentation, the so-called lactic acid fermentation. Malic acid from bacteria, contained in the red wine, is converted into milder lactic acid. Consequently, the sharpness content is reduced and the wine has a smoother and more full-bodied taste. Before the red wine is bottled, it matures in traditional wooden casks, small oak casks (Baroques) or in stainless steel casks. During that period, which can last many years, the wine changes and develops its characteristic taste by eliminating the smallest quantities of oxygen (fine oxidation).

AN OVERVIEW OF THE GENERAL PRODUCTION PROCESS:

GRAPE SEPARATION: The separation of the grapes from the stems is known as grape separation, or skinned grapes or combs. This separation leads to less tannin in the must and later in the juice.

RACKING: This is the process by which clear wine is separated from the settled elements, e.g. yeast.

ENRICHMENT: In Germany, the Wine Act of 1971 firmly prohibited the addition of sugar. Some exceptions are made for sugaring QbA-wines prior to fermentation, in order to raise the alcohol content.

BAR: Biological Acid Reduction takes place after alcoholic fermentation. It describes all chemical procedures carried out by microorganisms which convert the malic acid into

milder lactic acid by fostering the splitting-off of carbonic acid.

NEW WINE: The fermented grape must is called also "new wine" or "sweet cider." This piquant beverage with high yeast content can only be purchased directly from the winegrower.

FERMENTATION: Alcoholic fermentation is the conversion of sugar into alcohol and carbon dioxide. Fermentation is started by yeast existing naturally in the grape or by cultivated yeast added to the must.

YEAST: Unicellular, vegetable microorganisms capable of converting sugar into alcohol. Wine yeast consists mainly of *saccharomyces cerevisiae.*

SUBSTANCES IN THE CONTENT: All substances which come out in the wine including: alcohol, sugar rests, sharpness, tannin and color substances.

YOUNG WINE: Wine before filtration, which remains in yeast or which contains some yeast rests.

PRESSING: In the pressing process, the grapes or the must are squeezed to produce the must.

VINTAGE: Vintage or grape harvest is specified; it is the harvest period which is determined by the maturity of the grapes.

MUST: Ground and squeezed grapes, which contain the juice, are called must.

GRAPE JUICE: Squeezed juice from the grapes, intended for further wine processing.

APPLE JUICE WEIGHT: Measuring data uses the weight of apple juice as the standard, based on how much more 1 quart of apple juice weighs at the temperature of 68°F, than 1 quart of water. The apple juice weight is measured on the Oechsle-scale: four cups of apple juice, which weigh 2 lbs, has 70 grades Oechsle.

SUGAR RESTS: Unfermented sugar, which remains in the wine as "rest" after fermentation.

SHARPNESS: It comes out in the grape and later also in the wine as malic acid.

SWEET RESERVE: Unfermented grape juice used for sweetening the wines.

TARTAR: Harmless potassium cyanide in the form of tiny crystals, which arises as a result of alcohol formation and cooling after fermentation. Tartar presents no reason for complaint.

WHAT MAKES A GOOD WINE?

This is a difficult question for which there are two appropriate answers. First, the quality of the wine is determined according to four basic features of taste: fruit, alcohol, sharpness and sweetness. The balanced weight or the harmony of these components determines the quality of the wine.

The art of wine production lies, therefore, in balancing sugar and sharpness. Dry, sweet wines have a pleasant and mellow taste. An ideally balanced, sweet wine manages to be elegant and sweet, but not sticky.

FRUIT

There is a varying amount of fruit in every wine. The fruit of the wine is dependent on the type of grape which specifically affects the wine. Last but not least, the vineyard location and the maturity of the grapes in the course of the vintage also affect the intensity of the fruit. According to the vintage, the fruit in the wine can taste juicy and fresh. A specific aroma of fruit can markedly dominate the taste. On the other hand, it can also be very subdued. The fruit taste is usually complex and resembles a variety of fruit, the "fruit basket." Many fruit aromas have different nuances. Practice and experience will enable you to differentiate between them and to define the particular aromas as well as the various grades of maturity.

Alcohol

Alcoholic beverages exist internationally: from fermented mare milk in Siberia to rice wine in Southeast Asia to champagne in France and *pivo*, or beer, in the Czech Republic. The production formula is simple: everything that contains sugar can be fermented to become an alcoholic drink by adding yeast. When producing wine, sugar in the grape juice is brought to the fermentation stage through the use of natural or added yeast. The result is alcohol, mostly in the form of ethanol. This alcohol gives the wine its body and structure and determines the taste feelings on the palate. Wines high in alcohol content are mostly heavy and stodgy while wines with low alcohol content are light, elegant and finely fruity.

Sharpness

This word itself evokes an unpleasant feeling for many wine drinkers. However, sharpness decisively affects the character of the wine, grants it strength and completes its taste. A suitable sharpness is not only an indication of quality, but also of the chemical composition. The total sharpness in wine includes various types of sharpness, the most important being tartaric acid, malic acid and lactic acid. The sharpness comes mostly from the grapes and

The more sugar in the grapes, the higher the alcohol content can be.

only a small part is created during fermentation. Wines from colder regions usually contain more sharpness and piquant taste than wines from hot regions. With the maturing process, grapes lose their sharpness. Therefore, the winegrower's mastery lies in determining the right vintage time, when sugar and sharpness are perfectly balanced.

Wine contains mainly tartaric acid, malic acid and lactic acid. With fully mature grapes, the mild tartaric acids prevail.

SWEETNESS

At vintage time the grapes include glucose and fructose. The more mature the grapes, the higher the sugar content, which is fermented by yeast. Depending on the temperature or the amount of alcohol, the yeast can die off and the fermentation is finished. What is left of the desired sugar after fermentation is called "sugar rest." The sugar rest content is usually measured in ounces per quart and quantities are different from country to country. However contradictory it may sound, sweet is not equally sweet. The sweetness of a wine depends considerably on its corresponding sharpness. The blunter a wine, the more perceptible its sweetness.

It is possible to measure alcohol content and must weight. But analytical parameters say nothing about the real quality of the wine. The instruments we use to recognize a good wine are innate: the eyes, the nose, the tongue and the mouth. When we have trained our senses well, we can identify bad wines. Experienced tasters come to various

The Oechsle-grades are a measure of the total sugar content of the must.

conclusions when tasting the same wine. As a critical wine-taster, you will not be able to master all knowledge of wine. But trust your own taste and don't be discouraged. Of course, professionals have the advantage of previous experience and they can compare smells based on experience. There are different quality standards set by wine experts: balance, length, depth, complexity and typification. Naturally, however, these criteria for assessing the wine are subject to individual feelings. The more important thing is that you enjoy the wine! So keep tasting, in moderation and with common sense, of course! Practice makes perfect and the road to wine mastery is paved by many empty bottles.

With the so-called fermented wines, yeast has done the entire job – it has completely converted the sugar contained in the grape juice into alcohol.

Balance

Sweetness, sharpness, fruit and alcohol are the main components of wine. The four elements must be balanced and the more balanced they are, the better the wine.

Length

"Length" is an unmistakable feature of quality. A good wine should remain on the palate at least 20 or 30 seconds after swallowing. We refer to a "long consumption relish," a "long extension tail" or a "finale." All descriptions mean the same thing: the taste of the wine should last a long time!

DEPTH

A good wine should not taste insipid or one dimensional, but should have complex aromas and fine nuances which "bubble" below the surface and are released by "chewing the wine."

COMPLEXITY

A good wine should stimulate the senses and taste perceptions on different levels and in complex ways.

TYPIFICATION

This is one of the most difficult aspects of wine appreciation, which presupposes some experience. "Typification" is a way of classifying the aromas and taste nuances to be found in any good wine. For instance, Cassis aromas and tastes reminiscent of green paprika are typical features of the authentic Cabernet Sauvignon.

HOW DOES THE FRUIT GET INTO THE WINE?

Why exactly does Riesling smell of apple and peach and a Pinot Noir of mature cherries? It is simple: the same chemical compounds exist in wine as in fruits or vegetables. So far, 800 chemical compounds have been identified in wine. We can recognize these compounds as fruit or vegetables because they are stored, defined and assigned thus in the brain. Principally, our recollection of smell functions on a check-system base: the more smells and fragrances are stored, the quicker and more unequivocal is the retrieval of these smell samples. For example: the compound pyrazin exists both in green paprika and in Cabernet Sauvignon. Ethylprylat appears in both pineapple and in the Chardonnay grape. Pipernol compounds can be found both in peaches and also in the Riesling grape.

A recollection is often connected to a smell recognized from childhood experiences or holiday feelings. Sometimes smell and fragrances inspire melancholy moods. Wine aromas evoke many memories and impressions for us. Someone who has smelled black, mature cherries will quickly recognize this fragrance in the wine.

A pigeon hole system of flavors

Describing wines by their fragrances is a complicated task. The aromas in wine are composed of a wide variety of scents, which give a certain character of smell to the wine depending on its intensity. Besides the types of vine, soil and climate, we can also consider the individual location, the vintage and, not least the wine-grower's growing and cultivation methods.

The aromas in wine have various origins: Primary aromas result from the type of vine, climate and soil. Secondary aromas are formed during the fermentation, tertiary aromas come from maturing and storage.

When the nose perceives a smell, the correct words are often missing. How can a smell be aptly and accurately described? The best and the easiest way is to compare the smell with an already known smell. Walk around your garden, woods, fields, or town marketplace with an "opened nose:" sniff any flowers, trees, herbs or spices you encounter. Store your impressions and fill your recollection potential with various smells and tastes. Then discover the similarity of these smells with the fragrances in wine. Remember that the first impression of scent provokes the process of recollection. There is no absolutely standard way of smelling or method of scientifically orienting a wine or categorizing an impression: each person has his own perceptions and impressions.

THE MOST IMPORTANT FRAGRANCES IN WINE

PINEAPPLE

The fruit, which originated in Brazil, is also native to Asia and Africa. We come across slightly sweet pineapple fragrances in young white wine. This smell usually fades with the vintage of the wine. You can find the pineapple aroma in high quality wines, late vintages and even in wines from choice grapes left on the vine to dry out at the end of the season, as well as in Chardonnays from Burgundy, Australia and the United States.

Apple

The smell of apples is a key component of many white wines and champagnes because apples and grapes both contain a malic sharpness. In particular, Rieslings and Chardonnays have a distinct apple fragrance. On the other hand, the smell of overripe apples is regarded as sickly. If the juice runs through the malolactic fermentation, or acid decomposition, malic acid converts to lactic acid.

Apricot

Like the peach, the apricot comes from China. In wine, apricot fragrances smell more mature and concentrated than fine peach nuances. The fragrance is also favored by the noble rot botrytis cinerea. The range starts with dry white wines and proceeds to sweet noble wines and liquor wines.

Banana

The fragrance of mature bananas emerges from both white and red wines. In the vines of Gamay, Syrah or Chardonnay, you can always find subtle smells resembling bananas. Wines with a distinct banana aroma are best consumed young.

Pear

Around 1500 various kinds of pear are known today. The gentle pear aroma, often connected with the flavor of vanilla, can be found in many distinctly fruity liquors like white wines and champagnes. Pear aromas are very distinctive in Chardonnays from Burgundy, but also in mature Rieslings.

Bitter chocolate

The fundamental component of good chocolate is cocoa. The aroma of cacao contains around 500 various components, which are noticeably reflected in the wine. Chocolate or cocoa flavors are contained in mature red wines, mostly accompanied by subtle roast aromas, generated by the storage of the wine in small oak wood casks.

Blackberry

Blackberries belong to the family of the rose wines. The aromatic fruits taste juicy, sweet and simultaneously sharp in their optimal mature condition. The intense blackberry taste is distinct, recalling the aroma of conserved, mature black berries. Blackberry flavors are mostly found in complex red wines.

Butter

The flavor of fresh butter is discrete, but familiar to everyone. In wine, butter flavor comes out in the course of the lactic acid fermentation and is found in young, full-bodied

Chardonnays fermented in the Barriques. The feature has become common for the big white Burgrunder and the fat Chardonnays from South Africa, Australia and the United States.

PRUNE

The classic aroma of prunes develops during the fruit shrinking. A prune aroma comes out intensely, particularly with red wines from warm winegrowing regions. The heavy, slightly smoky flavor often resembles plum jam or marmalade.

STRAWBERRY

There are usually two strawberry flavors: the flavor of fresh fruit is especially typical of young red wines. Mature fruit aromas, which are reminiscent of strawberry jam, are found rather in older, complex red wines. We perceive strawberry flavors in fruity white wines.

MOWN HAY

What typically smells of "fresh hay" in young white wine and also in champagne is the fragrance of coumarin, which comes out in more than 30 various plants. The full aroma harmonizes ideally with fine fruit aromas.

Roasted bread

The flavor of fresh and roasted bread is standard in wine. Principally, one can find these aromas in white wines, for instance, Chardonnays or Sauvignons Blancs, which are fermented in the new oak casks. Chiefly, Chardonnays from Burgundy, Australia and the United States show in their youth distinct flavors of roasted bread.

Clove

The clove tree, which is native to the Indian Ocean, originally comes from the Moluccas. The spicy and distinct flavor of the clove is typical of mature and especially storable red wines, which also show flavors of cinnamon, nutmeg and pepper. In white wines, one can find clove flavors, in particular in mature spicy-traminers, but also in white wines from Bordelais or in the fine Sauternes.

Green paprika

The flavor of the green paprika is very distinct and it also partly resembles asparagus. The characteristic flavor is to be found in almost all wines from the grapes of Cabernet Franc and Cabernet Sauvignon, and it is regarded as typical of young Bordeaux-wines and their counterparts in America.

Honey

Honey and wine have been interconnected since ancient times. Wines are usually enriched by the aroma of honey. The flowery honey aroma resembles dried apricots, connected with flavor nuances of wax. The fine, slightly honey flavors come out in all quality wines and, provided that they are clear and flowery, they are a feature of the exceptional quality in wines.

Honeydew melon

The distinct flavor of the honeydew melon is noticeable in the Australian Chardonnay-wines, but also in sweet wines.

Coffee

Nowadays, coffee beans come mainly from Central and South America. The complex aroma contains about 850 different components. Chiefly, roast flavors can be found in fine scent substances in wines, which were aged in new, toasted wood casks. Old vintages of champagnes also show discrete coffee flavors.

Caramel
The caramel flavor resembles the classic toffees, which are produced from fresh milk, butter and cream. These fine caramel fragrances, which spread through many red wines from Bordelais and Burgundy, are a feature of refinement and elegance. Caramel is a term used in wine language to describe a color or flavor, which is chiefly assumed by old red wines.

Cherry
Sweet or sour, cherry is found in wine aromas. Young wines mainly remind you of the juicy cherry flavor you encounter in fully mature cherries. Cherry aromas are common flavors in older red wines.

Licorice
The licorice essence is gained from the licorice root, which tastes sweet and strong on the palate. Licorice flavors are

found mainly in red wines, rich in tannin, in the classic grapes Merlot, Cabernet Sauvignon and Pinot, which are aged in wood. It applies both to the great Bordeaux wines and also to red wines from the Rhône Valley and America.

Leather

Leather has its own specific smell commonly recognized in new leather products. We are dealing here with a blend of flavors, including the tannin plant, which is used for tanning animal skins. The leather flavor belongs among the so-called animal aromas and mainly comes out in older wines, such as Cabernet Sauvignon.

Almond

The oval fruit of the almond tree is available in sweet or bitter variations. Slightly bitter almond flavors are apparent in late Burgundy wines from slate soils, strong white wines or red wines with immature tannins.

Nutmeg

The aromatic nutmeg is the seed of the apricot-like nutmeg fruit, which exists in all tropical regions to the north or south of the equator. The best sorts come from the West Indies and Indonesia. Wines aged in wood or Barriques have a nutmeg flavor.

ORANGE

The orange comes originally from China and India. The refreshing aroma of orange contains fine, bitter substances, which harmoniously reflect its sweet flavor. High quality wines have orange aromas when a botrytis fungus infests the grapes. Grand Crus wines from Altenberg de Bergheim/Alsace are ranked among the most distinctive wines with orange flavor.

GRAPEFRUIT

The juice of the greatest citrus fruit smells refreshing, but also a little bit bitter. One can always recognize a touch of sulfur in its smell. The fine aromas of grapefruit come out in fresh, young Rieslings, Tokays, Pinot Gris, Chardonnays, but also in fine, high quality wines.

PEPPER

The aroma of (ground) pepper can be found in almost all great red wines in the world. The fragrance is subtle, not sharp, as is always supposed. In combination with fruit aromas, a harmonious fragrance arises, which discretely emphasizes the pepper, lending spiciness to the scent.

Peach
The sweet-smelling peach with soft skin originally comes from China. The gentle fragrance is typical of fresh, young white wines. Peach aromas are found in Riesling and champagne, often accompanied by a violet scent.

Roses/rosewater
The clear, intense aroma arises through the distillation of rose oil and is mostly used as an additive for pastry and cakes in the Asia. Rose water, however, can be found in drugstores and delicatessens everywhere. Rose aromas are particularly apparent in wines possessing a flowery scent such as Traminer, Yellow Muscatel, Spicy Traminer and Gray Burgundy.

Red currant
In botany, red currant belongs to the same genus as black currant. But in terms of fragrance, the slightly sour smell of red currant gives a fine feeling of freshness and sharpness. You can chiefly find this aroma structure in wines with the corresponding sharpness.

Black currant
This shrub plant is known for its black fruit and is common in red wines. The aroma is considered classic and represents a natural fruit concentration in the wine. The

warm, fruity aroma of black currants is found almost in all Pinot Noir wines from Burgundy, as well as in several Cabernet Sauvignon and Shiraz wines from America.

Tobacco

Tobacco aromas of various nuances – from fresh tobacco leaves to cut tobacco – are mostly found in older red wines aged in the Barrique.

Truffle

Truffles are fungi and grow underground, mostly in forest soil. Their intense and aromatic fragrance makes them a desirable rarity. Truffle aromas seldom come out in wines, yet they range from fresh Sauvignon Blanc to Loire and to Cabernet Sauvignon from Bordelais.

Vanilla

The vanilla pod originates in Mexico. Vanillin, perceptible in even a small concentration, is the main component of the scent. Vanilla flavor can be found in wines – white and red - aged in new oak casks (Barriques).

Violet

The edible petals of the violet are mainly used for aromatizing salads. Extracts from the peeled violet roots are suitable for ice cream, sugar and other confections. The aromatic violet smell is clearly recognizable in young red wines such as Beaujolais Primeur. Aromatic white wines have a violet aroma in the bouquet.

CINNAMON

Cinnamon is composed of the dried bark of the cinnamon tree, which grows in Sri Lanka and China. The slightly sweet, soft aroma with an oriental flavor comes out in wines aged in wooden casks. This cinnamon aroma can be found in wines such as Merlot from Bordelais or Shiraz from Australia, and in mature Sauternes, Tokay, Pinot Gris and natural spicy traminers.

LEMON

Lemon, the citrus fruit, is classically connected with sharp flavor, although true citrus sharpness is odorless. The subtle aroma of lemon is characteristic in fresh, sharp Rieslings from Germany and Alsace and in Sauvignon wines from France and America.

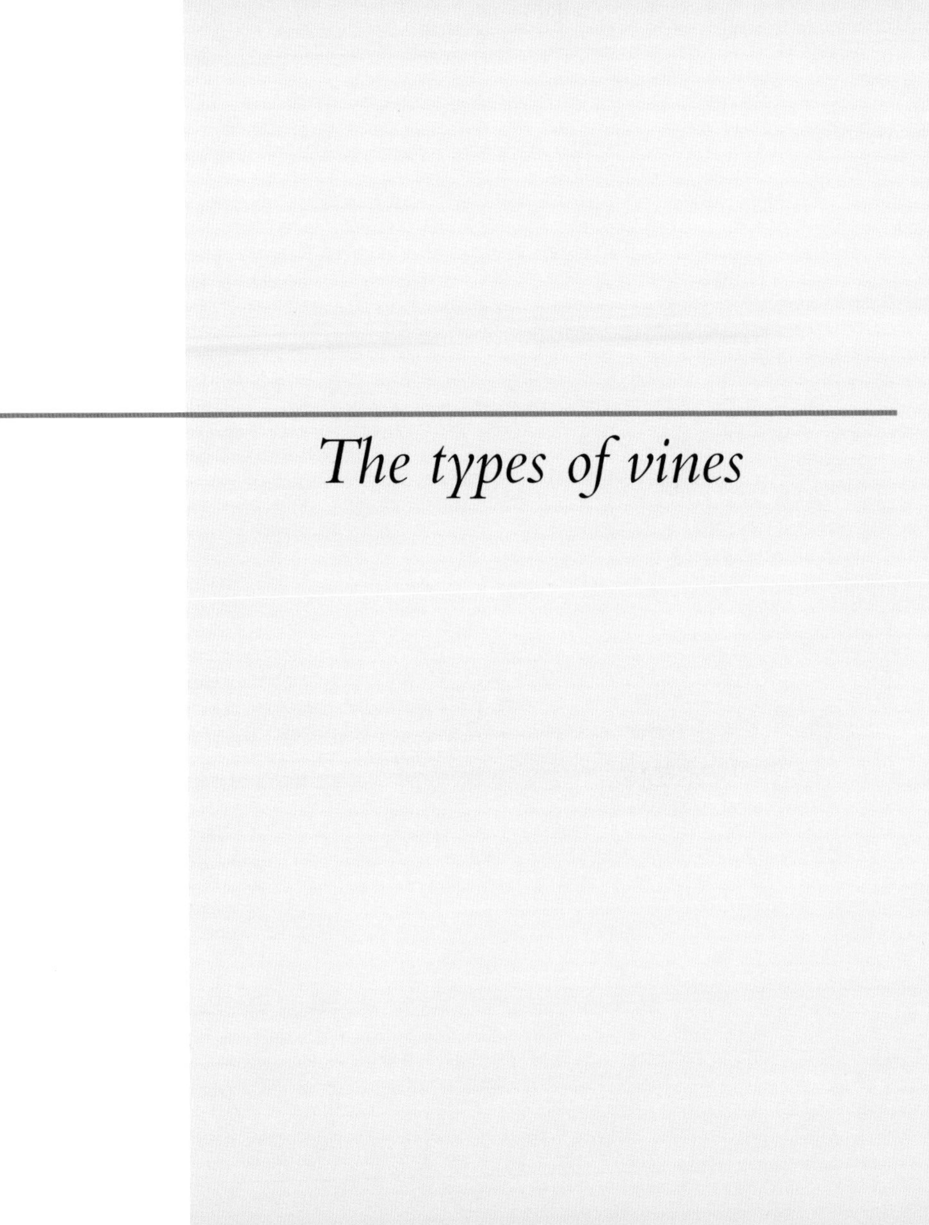

The types of vines

The types of vines

What flavor is each type of vine? It is a common question since there are around 10,000 types of vines. However, only some of them have become established worldwide. Certain types of vines are found in all winemaking areas around the globe. With the increasing internationalization of vines, climate and soil compatibility play a lesser role than the wine style, which represents the types of vine, and defines its further marketing.

Initially, the type of vine determines the character of the wine. It is the most distinct moment in the production of the wine and also it is the easiest feature to determine when tasting. The basic fragrance of the vine varies depending on conditions such as the soil, climate, water supply and the particular winegrowing methods of the winegrower.

The type of vine preserves its characteristics under many different conditions. As an allocation factor and identification feature, the vine becomes very important due to the increasing internationalism of wine consumption. Popular vine types are widely discussed and currently the fifty most common types make up almost 95% of the total production worldwide. Most of these successful vine types come from Europe and have proved their worth over the centuries before being brought to America. Some common vine types, at first unpopular among Europeans, suddenly achieved popularity in America and subsequently in Europe. Chardonnay, for example, followed a wave that came to Europe from America at the beginning of the 1990s and made the once unpopular wine very popular. Eventually certain winegrowers, particularly in Germany, worshipped it.

Famous red wines

BARBERA

The high yield and versatile red wine grape is especially popular in the warm winegrowing regions due to its acid content. In its home country, Piemont, Barbera grape cultivation takes up a decisive share of the grapevine area. These wines are relatively low in tannin and sharp, with a taste resembling sour cherries, cloves, tobacco and marmalade made of black and red berries. The range starts with light wines and progresses to young, spicy wines, followed by strong red wines. Barbera wines undergo a relatively long period of maturation in the cellar, aging in small oak wood casks which give the wine its characteristic spice and level off its sharpness.

Cabernet Franc

A very traditional French wine overshadowed by its mixed counterpart, Cabernet Sauvignon. In the winegrowing regions of Anjou-Touraine in the Loire valley and on the right Gironde shore in Bordelais, it has an advantage against its competitors. Compared with Cabernet Sauvignon, Cabernet Franc wines are brighter and lighter because of the discreet herbal taste of tannin.

Cabernet Sauvignon

The most famous and most common red Bordelais grapevine had already spread to the Old and New World long before it became fashionable at the end of the 18th century. The dark wines show a high content of tannin. They can be stored for a long time and mature very slowly. Richly fragrant, strong and classy, their taste resembles black currant, cedar and black pepper. The blends of mild types of vine such as Cabernet Franc, Merlot, Malbec and Petit Verdot produce very strong and distinct wines with a strong essence.

Carignan

This type of vine, whose growing area is five times bigger than that of Chardonnay, occupies the vineyards of southern Languedoc. Due to the late maturing of grapes, it thrives exclusively in warm climates such as Italy and Spain, California, Mexico and Israel. It is difficult to grow this vine and only carefully grown old vines produce the true character of Carigan wines. In some vineyards in Languedoc, especially in Roussillon, a white mutation, Carigan Blanc, can be found.

DOLCETTO

This vine is found exclusively in the provinces of Cuneo and Alessandria in Piemont. The acidic, deep dark wines have a special mild, full-bodied and fruity taste, as well as a fine aroma of liquorice and almonds. Dolcetto-wines should be consumed young. They taste best within the first two or three years. In Piemont, there are seven DOC areas for Dolcetto: Acqui, Alba, Asti, Diano d'Alba, Dogliani, Langhe Monregalesi and Ovada.

GAMAY

No other winegrowing area has such a perfectly designated type of vine as Beaujolais with its Gamay grape. Due to its high quality pulp, the official name of this type of vine is Gamay Noir á Jus Blanc. This type of vine, whose optimal growing conditions are in colder wine cultivation areas, develops buds very early and the grapes are consequently endangered by late frosts. As for the color, the wines are lighter and bluer than other red wines; they usually have a strong sharpness and a fresh aroma with banana, jam and acetone flavors.

GRENACHE

The second most common vine type in the world originates in Spain. The grape develops buds early and can develop strong sugar content. The wines are lighter than other red types of wine. Particularly in the French Rhône valley, this vine produces concentrated, savory and spicy red wines. In Australia, Grenache was the most common vine until the middle of the 1960s. However, it has been surpassed in part by Shiraz and Cabernet Sauvignon.

MALBEC

This very popular type of vine in Bordelais around fifty years ago is presently located mainly in Cahors in southwest France and in Argentina, where it is the most common dark vine type. The pure Argentinean Malbec (Malbeck) resembles Bordeaux in its style, although it lacks the elegant structure of wines from Bordelais. Malbec is also cultivated in Chile. Chilean wines contain more tannin than wines from Argentina. In small quantities, Malbec is grown also in northern Italy and in South Africa.

MEUNIER

This red vine type is among the most common types of vine in France and is used in the production of champagne. In total, this type of vine takes up 40% of the winegrowing areas of Champagne. Its high yield consistency and full-bodied character makes this Meunier grape relatively simple to cultivate along the chilly northern slopes in the wet valley of Marne. It owes its juicy flavor to the champagne blend and Pinot Noir and Chardonnay. In Germany, Meunier is known under the name Müllerrebe or Schwarzriesling.

MERLOT

In French Bordelais, the black blue Merlot grape is the most grown red type of wine. Merlot is grown mostly in the northeast winegrowing regions of Italy, but the New World has also discovered this full-bodied type of vine. In good locations, Merlot matures very early and brings relatively good yields, producing wines with high alcohol content. Pure Merlot wines are dark red and full-bodied with a particular, plum-like, spicy taste. On average, they achieve their maturity over a period of years.

NEBBIOLO

This type of vine goes back to the 13th century. The Nebbiolo grape produces the excellent Barolo and Barbaresco wines in the calcic marly soil in the DOCG areas. The refined grape from Piemeont yields relatively light-colored, but also tannin-rich, wines. The dry wines with an intense smell resemble dry roses and violets. Following several years of storing, they develop their sharp, tannin-rich aromas.

PINOT NOIR

Pinot Noir is among the oldest culture vines. Although it is demanding in terms of vineyard location and cellar technique, this type of vine, which originated in Burgundy, is native to almost all winegrowing regions of the world. Pinot Noir prefers a moderate climate and, consequently, is ill at ease in warmer grape cultivation areas. The most famous Pinot Noir wines come from Burgundy and have names such as Chambertin, Musigny, Pommard and Volnay. The wines are the deep red color of Burgrunder and this scent is reminiscent of black berries with a juicy sharpness.

SANGIOVESE

Among diverse variants – Brunello, Prugnolo Gentile and Morellino – Sangiovese is the most common red vine in Italy and is an integral member of the fine Tuscan red wine family. It is registered for the famous Brunello di Montalcino and is considered the foundation of Chianti, Vino Nobile di Montepulciano and a large number of the greatest Tuscan wines as well. It takes time before these wines develop their full aromatic potential. The intense ruby red, typically dry wines have a violet bouquet and a bitter taste.

SYRAH/SHIRAZ

The most famous Syrah wines grow in Côtes du Rhône – Hermitage – and in Côte-Rôtie. The Syrah grape is found in Châteauneuf-du-Pape and in other wines of the south Rhône, in Provence; Syrah is mostly mixed with Cabernet Sauvignon. In Australia, the grape has been known under the name Shiraz for centuries and is the most common red wine. In particular, the wines from Barossa Valley are regarded as first-class, quality wines. The wines are deep red, very rich in tannin and possess an interesting fragrant blend of violet, tobacco, truffle and liquorice.

TEMPRANILLO

The Tempranillo grape, the most renowned Spanish vine, is grown in Rioja Alta and in Rioja Alavesa. The thick-skinned grapes are pressed to produce dark, long-lived wines, which – unlike other Spanish wines – are not so alcoholic. The Tempranillo wines have a juicy flavor with a light raspberry touch and are usually relatively low in sharpness and light. As a result, Tempranillo is often mixed with sharper and daintier types of vines.

Prominent white wines

AUXERROIS

The classic French type of vine, mostly cultivated in the northeast of France, Luxembourg and Alsace, has a great deal of similarities to Pinot Blanc, with whose vines Auxerrois vines are often mixed. Provided that harvest yields are limited, this type of vine produces nutritious and particularly storable wines, with a fine honey taste in their bouquet, increasing with the vintage and resembling mature Chablis. In Germany, Auxerrois is solely grown in Baden.

CHARDONNAY

The wines from the Chardonnay grape are usually grown dry, so that they can emphasize the inflaming sharpness of this type of vine. Chardonnay wines form the basis for champagne. Despite their fresh, juicy, classy taste, these wines have an unpretentious and durable character, resembling not fully mature apples in taste. High quality Chardonnays are perfectly suitable for

aging in Barriques. The most well-known Chardonnay wines grow in Burgundy near Puligny-Montrachet, Meursault, Corton-Charlemagne and Chablis.

CHASSELAS

It is regarded as one of the oldest vine types. The Chasselas grape produces juicy, light wines almost all over the winemaking areas of the world. However, it has become important only in a few regions. Chasselas is found in Italy, North Africa, New Zealand and California as well as in Switzerland, cultivated as Gutedel, and in Austria, as Moster or Wälscher.

CHENIN OR CHENIN BLANC

This type of vine, originally from the Loire valley, is one the most versatile grapes in the world of winemaking. It produces fine and long-lived sweet white wines and is used as a wine blend in table wine production. There is a great spectrum of the Chenin grapevines, the most common type of vine in South Africa, which cover a large part of the winegrowing area in California as well. These pure wines usually have a refreshing, honey taste, reminiscent of the countryside and wet straw.

GREEN VELTLINER

The most significant vine type in Austria has regained respect in the recent years. In Niederösterreich, more than half of the total wine production falls to this high-yield and resistant type of vine. The range starts from the simple Zechwein to international high quality wines, in which a wealth of taste and substance are smartly and elegantly combined, and which resemble the great wines of Alsace. The typical green Veltliner is classically dry, with a slightly peppery, spicy taste and is best consumed within the first two or three years.

MACABEO

Also spread in French Roussillon and in Languedoc, it is the most common type of vine in northern Spain and is commonly used there as a blend of most of the AC-wines. This type of vine, which originally comes from the Near East, brings heavy yields and is relatively heat resistant. The wines have a distinctly floral aroma. However, they have a relatively weak sharpness. In the Spanish wine-growing regions, the grape is known under the name Viura and makes up around 90% of the total white wine production.

MARSANNE

This white type of vine has taken a great leap forward over the last years, both in Europe and America. Undoubtedly, its good yield potentials have contributed to its popularity. Marsanne emerges more often in the vineyards of French Midi and is grown as a full-bodied, distinctive pure wine. The wines are deep in color with a full almond aroma. Some of the oldest stocks of Marsanne in the world exist in Australia, particularly in Victoria.

Müller-Thurgau

The type of vine – a crossbreed of Riesling and Gutedel – is often scorned by connosieurs, but its vine is still the most commonly grown in Germany.

The relatively early maturing Müller-Thurgau is regarded as a high yield and light cultivating vine, usually producing rather simple wines. The flavorful, floral wines have a slight nutmeg flavor and are considered wholesome due to their relatively mild sharpness. The aromas resemble green apples, lemons, black currants, geraniums, nutmeg and green paprika. This precocious type is not suited for cultivation in America, but New Zealand possesses winegrowing areas of Müller-Thurgau.

Muscat Blanc À Petits Grains

The oldest and most high quality wine among the muscatel sorts has an exceptional concentration of fine aromas, similar to orange blooms and exotic spices. The smallest berries – as the name has it – vary in color from light to dark red. Besides the classic winegrowing area of France,

Muscat is increasingly cultivated in America and in Australia under the name Brown Muscat and Frontignac and in South Africa under the name Muscadel. In California, Muscat is mainly grown in the Central Valley.

PINOT BLANC

This French type of vine is a white mutation of Pinot Gris, a lighter version of Pinot Noir. No distinctions were made between Pinot Blanc and Chardonnay for a long time since they both are similar in their taste and often have a piquant, spicy bouquet, delicate almond touches and fine green apple aromas. While Pinot Blanc is produced throughout Central Europe, its growing center is situated in Alsace. In Germany, Pinot Blanc is known as Weissburgunder or Weissburgunder and in Eastern Europe it is grown under the name Beli Pinot. The wines are full-bodied, occasionally elegant and can mature to the highest quality grades.

RIESLING

The small round Riesling grape is the queen among white wines, due largely to its flexibility, for there is no other vine which covers such a large quality spectrum as Riesling. The relatively high content in sharpness makes it almost unlimitedly storable. The same particularly applies to high quality, sweet Riesling wines, such as those made from specially selected grapes or sweet wines made from grapes exposed to frost, which belong to the specialties of this type of vine. Late-maturing vines produce particularly fine, elegant wines in chilly wine-making areas. Riesling wines remain astonishingly refreshing over decades. In its bouquet, Riesling resembles vineyard peaches, apples, grapefruits, rose blossoms, honey and fresh grass. Except for Germany, Austria and Alsace, where it is prominent and celebrated, in other countries Riesling plays only a subordinate role.

SAUVIGNON BLANC

This French vine, also found in America, produces characteristic, dry white wines. The full-bodied Sauvignons have a strong aroma, with a very refreshing touch, resembling green fruits. Fragrance substances such as passion fruit, citrus, red currant and asparagus often accompany the aroma. Aging in small wooden casks (Barrique) can pleasantly intensify the juicy character. Sauvignons show less freshness and full-bodied character only in the warmer wine-growing areas of the Southern Hemisphere.

SÉMILLION

The Sémillion grape, whose origin lies in southwest France, is typically found in America. While Sémillion has a rather grassy taste when grown in chilly New Zealand, Australia and the State of Washington, Sémillion wines from Chile are voluminous and strong. In Europe, Sémillion plays a role in France, where it is registered as a dry, white wine. In a blend with Sauvignon Blanc, this type of vine forms an important part of Sauterne, one of the long-lived sweet wines of the world.

VIOGNIER

Condrieu is probably the best-known wine pressed from the Viognier grape. The deep, dark yellow grapes lend this wine a strong color. Relatively high alcohol content and a fragrant floral aroma with hints of apricot and peach have made Viognier famous. Aside from France, where Viognier stocks continually increase, there are a few vineyards in Australia. The scarce white wines from the Viognier grape should be drunk young, when their unusual taste is most distinct.

Wine producers & wine regions

Wine producers & wine regions

Whether a classic or a newcomer, wine has become an international article of commerce, and the variety of wines cultivated internationally has never been as immense as it is today. While a few decades ago, traditional European wine nations, such as France, Italy, Germany and Spain dominated the stage, now America has found its position on the international market. By means of huge investments and a healthy pioneer spirit, the overseas countries have made enormous progress in quality. Quick transport routes allow wines to travel to faraway markets. Wines from America find their way to Europe and the other way around: one hundred-year-old traditions of classic wine-making countries meet the innovative styles of relatively young winemaking countries – an interesting combination which introduces the consumer to a varied wine world and new taste experiences. Although many of these wines are made from the same type of vine, the results are not mere copies of European wines. On the contrary, the wines differ greatly in flavor and aroma because of the diversity of climates and soils in which they grow.

EUROPE AND AMERICA

EUROPE

- Terroir with empirical values from centuries as a unique phenomenon
- Mostly small, individual winemaking estates which produce their own grapes
- Wide variety
- Production of storable wines
- Traditional wood and Barrique aging
- Conditioned by strong climate variations which affect vintage
- Image and market advantage lent by long tradition
- High degree of quality regimentation and classification

AMERICA

- Big wine companies determine the market
- Multi-district blends – production of particular wine styles in great quantities
- Buying more grapes on a large scale than common in Europe
- Concentration of the production of less internationally renowned types of vine
- Production of wine brands for fast consumption
- Relatively stable climate
- Up-to-date cellar technologies, supported by application of the latest production procedures
- More favorable production costs

Germany

The German winegrowing areas are situated near the 51st degree of latitude, which is regarded as the farthest northern climate border for growing vines. Influenced by a relatively cold continental climate – warm summers, cold winters – the grapes mature very slowly and are usually harvested only in the middle of October. The total winegrowing area amounts to around 260,000 acres, ranking Germany among the smaller winemaking nations. The wine styles are as varied as the soil structure and winemaking locations. Germany, which can look back at its brilliant and successful winegrowing history, is considered the country of Riesling. About 20% of the winemaking area is planted with Riesling, which has symbolized the quality of German wines in Germany and abroad over the last 200 years.

The German quality pyramid in ascending order: table wines, quality wines of specific cultivated areas (QbA), Kabinett-wines, late vintage, selection, and wines made from specially selected grapes (BA), dry wines from specially selected grapes (TBA) and Eiswines.

AHR

The word "Ahr" evokes the thought of deep red, elegant wines, which have made the winegrowing area between the 50th and 51st degree of latitude a "small paradise." Ahr is ranked with Klosterberg and 43 others among the wine regions in northern Europe. However, elegant Spätburgunder wines grow here, which have boomed im-

mensely in recent years and have given noticeable profits to the German red wine world. The valley of the Ahr, whose wine history can be traced back 1000 years, lies between the Eifel and the Rhine. Right after the Second World War, the vine cultivation area along the Ahr was twice as large as it is today. The hard soil structure was difficult for many wine-growing companies. Most of the vineyards are on steep locations, which are not only difficult to cultivate, but expensive to purify. Only a small part – around 15% of the vine area – is located on the terraced slopes and only 10% of the vineyards are situated on the plain. Yet, the valley of the Ahr offers the vines an ideal climate and growing conditions. While deep loess soils dominate in the lower valley of the Ahr with their basalt deposits and garden countryside, giving a soft and tender character to the wines, weathered slate and sandstone define the soils of the middle valley of the Ahr.

The warmth amassed between the narrow rock walls of the Ahr Valley acts as an oven. The cloven rocks and the slate soil absorb the heat, reflecting the sun's warmth on the vines. Additionally, the Eifelberge Mountains nearby protect the steep and terraced vineyards located in the cloven, middle valley of the Ahr from cold winds and too large temperature variations. Almost like a hothouse, the vineyards are exposed to the Mediterranean climate on the Ahr, with its enormously high average temperatures, even in this latitude on the northern edge of winemaking country.

The Spätburgunder grapes cover 608 acres, almost half the winegrowing area. Although Ahr red wines still possess a distinct, lingering sweetness, the dry, ruby red, elegant wines with a fine aroma are increasingly well-known. "Ahrburgunder" wines are more often aged in small wood casks. However, these should not be compared with the classic red wines from Burgundy. The selection of nutritious Spätburgunder is a regional specialty. The Portuguese grape produces lighter and brighter red wines, best drunk cold in the summer; the Domina grape – a blend from Portuguese Spätburgunder – delivers sharp red wines.

Another white wine, Riesling has its place in the valley of the Ahr. On an area of about 124 acres, Riesling grapes are predominantly formed by little humus on the steep slopes facing the south. The Riesling wines have an enticing, floral sharpness, compared to the wines from the Müller-Thurgau grapes. Ahr wines store well – aside from some exceptional, quick, ready-to-drink Portuguese wines. However, hardly any older vintages can be found. This winegrowing area is experiencing enormous demands because of the relatively small harvest quantities and most of the cellars are emptied. Of the 900 winegrowing estates, around 80% of the winemakers, some possessing less than one hectare of vinegrowing area, have united themselves into a winegrowers' organization. Six wine producers from Ahr are members of the association called Verband Deutscher Prädikats- and Qualitäts-Weingüter (VDP). There is also a bigger state-owned company with an affiliated regional training school and research institute in Marienthal with 50 acres.

MOSEL-SAAR-RUWER

Hardly any other German winegrowing areas show such a distinctive wine quality as the traditional Riesling from the Mosel, Saar and Ruwer. The top wines from Mosel, Saar and Ruwer have always been ranked among the best-known German wines and have never lost their respected reputation in Germany and abroad. They owe their eminence to the traditional unions such as "Grosser Ring VDP," "Bernkasteler Ring" and "Ruwer Riesling," whose auction sales and wine presentations have left their mark on the positive image of the winegrowing area. The Mosel-Saar-Ruwer wine region, squeezed between Hunsrück and Eifel, ranks among the northern winegrowing regions. The soils in the Rhine Schiefergebirge on the Obermosel are typical of muschelkalk, slate weathering and trias, whereas Devon slate dominates the terroir in the valleys of Saar and Ruwer. The Saar and Ruwer wines acquire steely, honed sharp-

ness, which comes out in the wines of Mittelmosel. South of the famous area of Mosel, in Zell, the grapes are grown in soft silica sandstones, which give slender, fine juicy elegance to the Riesling. The valley locations of the winegrowing area consist of gravel, pea gravel and sand layers.

Although there is an optimal amount of rain falling on the steep slopes and valleys, the relatively low number of sunny days does not make it possible for the grapes to mature every year. A vintage list from 1848 to 1947 shows that roughly only a third of the vintages can be marked satisfactorily.

But in the last years, the climate situation has changed positively. The vintages from 1988 to 1997 were all qualitatively awarded due to improved winegrowing methods. The prolonged maturation period in the vineyard allows the Riesling wines in particular to obtain their consistent elegance and long life. Mosel wines are trendy, for they are light and despite their variety, they contain less than 10% of alcohol.

Although the winemaking area is named after three rivers, the Mosel dominates the wine stage. Geographically, this area forms a winemaking unit, stretching along the considerable length of the Mosel River. Riesling determines various variants in the six winegrowing areas which cover the area of the mouth of the Mosel to the Rhine upstream. In total, the vine area on the Mosel, Saar and Ruwer covers 30,150 acres, divided into 20 large and 524 single locations and cultivated by 9000 companies. The average size of a company is about 3.5 acres, which has to do with the considerably difficult growing situation. Over 50% of the grapes are on steep slopes, which is more than in any other German winegrowing area. Cultivation is difficult and expensive. Around 1500 man-hours are necessary to cultivate 2.5 acres of the vine area on the Mosel. In Pfalz, the number of hours is less than half. Machines can only approach a small part of the vineyards and the funicular drive is used in roughly one third of the vine area for cultivating the soil and during the harvesting period. Many smaller winegrowing estates have joined the winegrowers' organizations, which barely market 25% of all Mosel-Saar-Ruwer wines.

The term "steep slope-Steillage" has been recently introduced officially as an indication of quality. Due to the difficult conditions in these locations, the area was granted a special status under certain conditions. What is qualified as high-quality German white wines in some regions is often late vintage quality on the Mosel. Until 1983, winegrowers were allowed to improve their wines by adding up to 10% sugar water to the must. The young generation of winegrowers from Mosel, Saar and Ruwer have ventured into modern marketing. With "Selection Mosel 2000," "Top Leiwen Selection" or "Riesling Pomaria," new qualities were created, promoting full-bodied Mosel-Riesling. Riesling has a 55% share of the vineyards in Platzhirsch. The world famous center of Riesling is Mittelmosel with a big S-loop between Kinheim and Lieser.

Müller-Thurgau has won 22% of the vine area and its grapes are mostly in the valley areas. Elbling is still popular and has a 10% share in Obermosel and is marketed as a pure wine; it produces piquant, light wines with a high level of sharpness. The kerner grape, which is similar to Riesling, has considerably higher yields and appears to have good chances on the Mosel.

MITTELRHEIN

This German winemaking region offers the nicest and most romantic setting for winemaking. In the valley of the Rhine, in the area between Bingen and Lahnstein, most vineyards are situated high over the river on the picturesque vine terraces between the medieval castles and palaces. It is no wonder that Mittelrheintal has been put on the UNESCO cultural heritage list.

The sales of high quality wines from Mittelrhein are not exclusively due to nostalgia and romanticism connected with the Rhine, although a great part of the trade is indeed realized by tourists in the frequently visited local restaurants in the summer. Small, independent companies dominate the wine market. Here, you can find the proper Rhine wine, regarded as the purest Riesling some decades ago. Today, this name represents almost all wines growing near the Rhine.

The center of winemaking in Mittelrhein near Bacharach, in the so-called "4-valley area," covers half of the cultivated area along the Rhine and the adjacent valleys. Unfortunately, the cultivated area of Mittelrhein is getting smaller each year. At the end of the century, more than 5,000 acres were cultivated. Today there are only barely 1,600 acres left. Divided into two areas, 11 large areas and 111 single areas, the total does not even represent 1% of the total German vine cultivation area. This dramatic decline in cultivated area is not only due to the difficult and costly cultivation of the steep slopes, but also to the need to secure the area with expensive walls.

Many winegrowers have successfully fought for useful land purification and today they let their separated and often-inaccessible areas go fallow. In spite of the divided state of vineyard ownership, the winegrowers' organizations do not play a decisive role in Mittelrhein, since they market barely 25% of the wines through cooperatives.

70% of the winegrowers sell their wine from their own overheads. Many of these small, independent family com-

panies have made enormous progress in growing wine and cellar economy in recent years– despite the high production costs on the steep slopes. The finest, most elegant and expressive full-bodied wines come from these vine slopes on the Rhine or from small, adjacent slopes. In addition, convenient climate conditions make up for the difficult geologic conditions. The mountains on both sides of the Rhine protect it from cold winds, allowing plentiful sunbeams to fall on the slopes. The water surface reflects additional warmth. The character of the wines – Müller-Thurgau, Kerner and Spätburgunder as well as 75% Reisling – is determined by the various soil sorts.

Essence wines come from the heavy loess soils in the lower Mittelrhein near Leutesdorf.

The heavy weathered soils on the steep slopes produce extra rich wines. Around Boppard, elegant Riesling, often with a distinct residual sweetness, grows in the slate rock soils. The typical, dry wines come from the soil near Bacharach and Steeg, which is mixed with pure Devon slate. In the area of the Siebengebirge, the soils are of the volcanic origin and give a mineral, slightly acidic character to the reddest Spätburgunder and Portugieser wines. The taste of most of wines from Mittlerhein improves when they are given one or two years to reduce their sharpness and develop their full maturity.

RHEINGAU

Between Hochheim and Lorchhausen, where the Rhine changes its course and continues from the east to the west, we find the cultivation area Rheingau. Surrounded by the woody upper reaches of the Taunus and Rhine, the villages and towns with their famous vineyards are located along the broad current like a string of beads. This region is an ideal place for vine cultivation, especially since all the vines face south, guaranteeing the best sunbeams. The Taunus offers enough protection from the harsh northernt winds. The Rhine, as broad half a mile in some places, reflects the sun beams and provides warm and humid absorption and a relatively stable temperature.

In addition, according to the new wording of the German Wine Act of 1971, five great areas were supposed to be created in an area called Johannisberg in Rheingau. The idea met with firm resistance from traditional winemaking communities. Today, Rheinrau has ten large growing areas with a total of 118 single areas. The various soils offer optimal conditions for growing vines: in the higher locations, particularly in the steep vineyards between

Rüdesheim and Lorchhausen, slate, quartz and sandstone guarantee special, classy, powerful wines.

In the lower vine slopes, you find deep and limy loess soils, in which essence and full-bodied wines are grown. These are ideal conditions for Riesling, which dominates 80% of the total vine cultivation area of 8,150 acres in Rheingau. Rheingauer wines, which have become very well-known, are high quality: selection wines, wines made from specially selected grapes, dry wines and sweet wines made from grapes which have been exposed to frost, are accompanied by full, juicy, natural sweetness and sharp aroma varieties. These long-lived wines have experienced a breathtaking renaissance and sell for record prices at world auctions. Kloster Eberbach, Schloss Johannisberg and Schloss Vollrads have made such wine cultivation famous. The names Kabinett (German high quality wine) and late vintage were used here for the first time as a quality feature. With the latest bottle classification (around 3,385 acres) and the introduction of the quality mark "first wine" in 1999, Rheingau has again taken the lead in German winegrowing.

In Rheingau, there are 1500 winegrowing estates, mostly independent sellers, whose quality structure has altered considerably over the last years. While the traditional high quality wines have fallen to a middle position, the relatively small, young family companies have overtaken the leading position of the region. Winegrowers' organizations play a diminished role in Rheingau and market exactly 15% of the annual wine quality. Approximately half

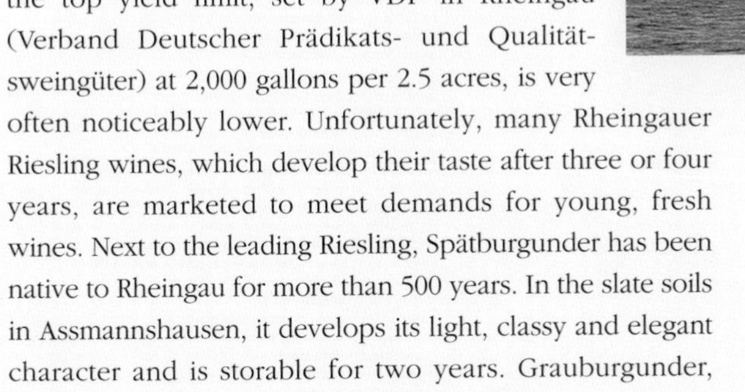

of the Riesling wines are exported, although the share of residual sweet wines has increased at the expense of full, dry, sharp Riesling. The future marketability of sharp Riesling wines internationally is a competitive subject in Rheingau.

Nonetheless, companies reduce the hectare yields by selective harvests, so that the maximal wine quality is achieved with healthy vines. Still, the top yield limit, set by VDP in Rheingau (Verband Deutscher Prädikats- und Qualitätsweingüter) at 2,000 gallons per 2.5 acres, is very often noticeably lower. Unfortunately, many Rheingauer Riesling wines, which develop their taste after three or four years, are marketed to meet demands for young, fresh wines. Next to the leading Riesling, Spätburgunder has been native to Rheingau for more than 500 years. In the slate soils in Assmannshausen, it develops its light, classy and elegant character and is storable for two years. Grauburgunder, Kerner and, since the beginning of the 1980s, Chardonnay have been grown in smaller quantities in Rheingau.

NAHE

The small Nahe River, which flows into the Rhine near Bingen, has given this cultivated area its name. From the river's mouth, upstream to the little town of Kirn, vine slopes line the river valley, as well as the adjacent valleys Guldenbach, Gräfenbach, Glan and Alsenz. The area of Nahe – the cultivated area covers around 11,400 acres – is a relatively young wine region. From 1950 to 1975, the cultivated area doubled. However, only after the amendment of the German Wine Act of 1971, were the boundaries of the cultivated area exactly defined. Until then, the Nahe wines were sold under the inclusive term, Rhein wine. Since 1993, the cultivated area of Nahe has consisted of Nahetal, divided into seven large areas and 328 single areas.

The taste nuances of the wines are very versatile due to the varying soil structure; further, the wines are marked by three different terroirs: in the north, there is a broad stretch of slate and sandstone in the soil. Strong, classy wines grow near the large area Schlosskapelle around Bingen. Further to the south, in the direction of Bad Kreuznach, sand, marl and loam produce full-bodied and elegant wines. The soil contains a high share of loess soil where full-bodied wines grow. To the west and north of Nahe, clay shale determines the soil. The wines there are mostly floral and durable with a decent sharpness. In the nearby area between Bad Münster and Schlossböckelheim, the terroir is of volcanic origin, interspersed mainly with porphyry and leach. The soil often suffers from drought in the hot summer months, owning to the meager moisture that it is equipped to absorb. The wines from these soils show much sharpness and fine mineral fragrances. The wines from the upper course of the Nahe River are often compared with Mosel wines. In the lower course, they are referred to as the Rheingauer type. For a long time, most of the tasty Nahe wines were grown there. Today, more dry wines are grown in all parts of the seven large areas.

Nahe wines are sharp, classy and have surpassed Müller-Thurgau in popularity. They are astonishingly durable and vintages from the 1970s are still at the height of their flavor. The once popular Nahe-Silvaner has dropped markedly, but is still cultivated in 10% of the total area; on the other hand, Kerner grapes and Scheugrapes have caught on nicely. The Bacchus grape has made its career in the area of the Nahe.

Apart from a series of great, renowned estates, medium-sized family companies determine the wine in this area. Almost half of the wines are sold directly as bottle wines by producers. Winegrowers' organizations market about 20% of the annual production.

Yield reduction in the vineyards and modern cellar technology are the beginning of the production of the high quality wines. Moreover in 1997, the very active Verband der Prädikatsweingüter (VDP) passed a new and strict classification of its wines: the names of the area are only permitted for Riesling wines. All other wines – including those from the top areas – are allowed to take the names of the local estates. The maximum yield is limited to 1,300 gallons per 2.5 acres and all wines must be tasted blind. These are strict rules, not universally agreed upon, but achieve their goal in the end. Rieslings from Nahe finish first on lists of the German wines.

RHEINHESSEN

Confusion and contradictions about the greatest German grape cultivation area start with the name: Rheinhessen is not situated in the state of Hessen, but in Rheinhald-Pfalz. About 30% of the agriculturally useful areas are planted with grapes, divided into 23 large areas and 432 single areas. In Rheinhessen, there are only three municipalities without vineyards in their cadastral areas. However, in the hilly area, protected against the cold winds by the heights of the Pfälzer Bergland, Hunsrück and Taunus, the vineyards are scattered and interrupted by arable lands.

Many winegrowers prefer quantity to quality in Rheinhessen. Every fourth bottle of German bottled wine comes from the large grape sea of about 65,500 acres; high quality wines are rare, although their share is increasing. However, changing an image is a protracted process. The cultivated area near the Rhine bend is given by the points of Worms, Bingen and Mainz and is always connected with the most famous type of wine "Liebfrauenmilch."

The variety of vines makes identifying Rheinhessen wines very difficult: more than 30 sorts are grown, along with another 20 different types of vine in extensive single areas. The classic types of wines: Müller-Thurgau, Silvaner and Riesling have been superseded by new varieties over the past years, bringing relatively high yields and good quality even during a bad harvest. Today, half the varieties of all new cultivation are red. Yet, Riesling is still popular and Silvaner has experienced a renaissance.

The Rheinhessen's high quality still comes from Rheinfront. Some of the best Riesling wines grow here on perlite and clay shale. In addition, the loess soil determines the soils of the rest of the cultivated area. Around 8000 winegrowers' estates market just 3 % of the total quantity. On the other hand, about 65 % of the wine business is carried out by vintners and about one third of the wines are exported. The young winegrowers' generation has said goodbye to the "sweet" past of the Rheinhessen wines and increasingly produces dry wines. The "Rheinhessen Selection" requires pure, dry Riesling, Silvaner or Grauburgunder wines, which are partly offered without area and high quality brands. "Rheinhessen Silvaner RS," a dry wine, which has been on the market since 1986, is exclusively sold by producers. Many other winegrowers who do not

participate in marketing actions, reduce dramatically the high yield, pick manually and selectively and invest a lot into up-to-date cellar technologies in order to achieve the desired quality.

Pfalz

The second largest German cultivated area is smaller than the neighboring state of Rheinhessen, presenting almost 6,000 acres of the vineyards. From the southern edge of Rheinhessen near Worms to the French border, the strip of Pfalz grapes stretches over the long, narrow stretch of land. The grape zone runs parallel with the Rhine, but does not reach its shore. The area is divided into Südliche Weinstrasse and Mittelhaardt/Deutsche Weinstrasse. The dividing line is near Neustadt. In total, there are 25 large areas and 330 single areas divided into about 150 winegrowing places. The German vineyards are closely situated in the cultivated areas on the edge of the Haardt, the hilly offset of the Pfälzer Wald. The mild climate has an almost southern character along this strip of land. Where almonds, figs and hesperidia mature on the wind-protected slopes, the grapes also have convenient growth conditions. The fertile soil, interspersed with loess, new red sandstone, Muschelkalk, marl, granite and slate is reflected in all of the Pfalz wines. In the area of Südliche Weinstrasse, grapes grow mainly in lime and loess soils. The wines taste juicy, harmonic and completely sharp, resembling the Alsace wines. Even during droughts, the soil stores up enough moisture to keep the wines astonishingly fresh and full-bodied in dry vintages. In the northern areas of Südliche Weinstrasse, the soils are much sandier and leakier. Elegant and juicy white wines grow there as well as mild and rich red wines.

The area of Mittelhaardt/Deutsche Weinstrasse encompasses around 27,000 acres of vineyards. The soils are slightly lighter, as in Südliche Weinstrasse, and they mostly consist of sand, clay, new red sandstone and basalt. The wines from this terroir are often juicy and elegant. Zellertal on the north edge of Pfalz is known for its full-bodied, extract rich wines.

Riesling dominates the vine variety in this cultivated area, taking up 22% of the cultivated area in Pfalz. Mittelhaardt, in particular, whose estates grow an 80% share of Riesling, is the land of Riesling. The share of Müller-Thurgau grapes is 20% of the total area, with a falling tendency. In Südpfalz, Grau and Weissburgunder wines are strongly cultivated, as well as Chardonnay. The cultivated area of Silvaner has dropped markedly from 50% to 7%. On the other hand, red wine wins more friends also in the area of Pfalz. Ten years ago around 6,200 acres were cultivated for grapes. The number has since almost doubled. At the same time, the Barrique cultivation in Pfalz underwent a substantial boom.

Many smaller family companies, but also the large famous traditional estates market their wine directly to the final consumers and the domestic gastronomy. The twenty-six Pfalz winegrowers' organizations process around 14,085 acres of grapes and serve the on-line businesses and food industry.

HESSISCHE BERGSTRASSE

This cultivated area, which is barely 1,100 acres in size, lies between Darmstadt and Heppenheim. Hessische Bergstrasse is at least 50 times smaller than the vine area of Rheinhessen. It was only in 1971, in the course of the reformation of the German Wine Act, that Hessische Bergstrasse obtained the status of an independent cultivated area. The people of Baden integrated their vineyards along Bergstrasse into their Baden cultivated area and the winegrowers from Hessische Bergstrasse did not want to join Rheingau. And so Hessische Bergstrasse came into being and today covers three large and twenty-four single areas. It was not until the Reunification of Germany, when the central German wine-growing regions of Sachsen and Saale-Unstrut were added, that Hessische Bergstrasse became the smallest German cultivated area. Only 0.3 % of all German wines are grown there and most of the 800 companies are part-time winegrowers, who only tend of their vineyard and cellars at the end of the day. Two winegrowers' organizations, in Gross-Umstadt and in Heppenheim, farm a total of around 700 acres; the largest single company is the state winegrowers' estate in Bensheim with around 100 acres.

The wine quantity in Hessische Bergstrasse is so small that most of the wines are only drunk locally. Hessische Bergstrasse is a popular recreational area for Rhein-Main due to its especially mild climate. While in some other regions, winter temperatures remain, the almond trees are beginning to blossom in the western offsets of Odenwald. In addition to the advantageous climate, there are also geological advantages: embedded between the Neckar, Rhine and Main, most of the vineyards are situated on downward sloping hillsides facing west from the Odenwalden. While the ridges of the Odenwald protect the grapes from cold wind storms, the vineyards enjoy optimal sunbeams on the relatively steep slopes. Besides the vineyards between Seeheim and Heppenheim, there is also the so-called "Odenwälder Weininsel" near Gross-Umstadt in the northeast. The light soils made of a mixture of weathered rocks and juicy loess warm up quickly, the green vineyards store plentiful rain and provide sufficient moisture for the deep-rooted grapes.

Demanding Riesling wines find ideal conditions there. Around 55% of the cultivated area of 1,100 acres is high quality grape land. The wines are mostly grown dry and show their prickling varieties. Bergsträsse-Riesling wines reach their maximum flavor only after two or three years of storage. Silvaner and Müller-Thurgau varieties: Little Traminer Gewürztraminer and Weissburgunder, grown along the Hessische Bergstrasse, are worth mentioning, even though they are not common to this region. Red wines such as Spätburgunder and Portugieser are scarce in the area of Bergstrasse. The last harvest years, in particular the perfect vintage of 1997, showed that even in modestly cultivated areas, high quality wines mature. What is astonishing is the high share of wines made from specially selected grapes. Eiswines have been offered in Hessische Bergstrasse since 1977.

FRANKEN

Along the Main, from Aschaffenburg to Hassfurt, stretches the great Franconian winegrowing area, more than 15,000 acres in size. Although the cultivated land is scattered across a vast territory, the wine area of Franken is divided into three areas, 23 large areas and 216 single areas: the main part is situated in the triangle of the Main and around Würzburg. The most renowned German vineyards are lo-

cated on "muchelkalk" soil: Würzburger Stein, Escherndorfer Lump und Randersackerer Pfülben. To the north of Würzburg, a small winegrowing area around Hammelburg is located on the Franconian Saale, part of the triangle of the Main. In Steigerwald near Kitzingen, the vines are situated on the nice, sunny southwestern slopes. The fertile Triassic soil stores up and guarantees enough moisture even during dry years. The highest weights of the must are usually achieved here, especially in the vineyards on the southwestern offsets of the ridges near Iphofen and Rödelsee. The countryside in the lower Main, the so-called triangle of the Main between Aschaffenburg and Miltenberg, is influenced differently by geology and climate. In the western area, on the steep slopes along the small Kahl River, some of the most elegant Franconian Riesling wines are grown. Around Klingenberg, where red sandstone detines the soil, not only distinctively sharp white wines are grown, but also Spätburgunder wines and red sorts dominate the new variants. Barely 5% of all Franconian wines are red wines, for example some types of Portugieser und Spätburgunder wines. The Franconian wine land is determined by the advantages and disadvantages of the continental climate: while the dry, hot summers stand to the grapes' credit, early cold and fall temperatures bring out frost in the vineyards. Traditionally, Franconia was a land of Silvaner, but this has completely changed over recent years. Today, more than a half of all Franconian wines are from the Müller-Thurgau grape and are classier and more full-bodied than in other cultivated areas, due to the soil and climate. Silvaner develops its harmony of power and elegance in the Muschelkalk soil and still takes up around 20% of the total cultivated area. Kerner and Riesling wines come third or fourth in the range of vine types. Franconian winegrowers like experimenting and you can also find new variants such as Rieslaner, Bacchus, Albalonga, Mariensteiner, Ortega, Morio-Muskat and Scheurebe, all of which are excellent, high quality wines.

Such a selection of wines makes it hard to achieve a late vintage, compared to the classical sorts. The demands for quality wines from Franconian winegrowers are still high. The middle grade for the maturity of the grapes is not exceptionally high, but the Franconian winegrowers have special demands for extract wines. Only the high quality wines are filled into the classic wide, rounded bottles. Half of the annual vintage is marketed by the seven Franconian organizations. Besides the large, traditional winegrowers' estates in Würzburg and Castell, smaller family companies are winning more and more terrain.

WÜRTTEMBERG

In the cultivated area of Württemberg, everything is completely different. Winegrowers' organizations determine the market and produce almost 80% of the total wine quantity per year. Part of it stays in the region or is consumed by the Swabians. After all, it comes from an area of 27,000 acres. Besides the large central organizations, there are about 62 local organizations offering all wines from the region and selling them through their own wine shops and points of sale. The cultivated area of Württemberg, divided into six areas, with 17 large and 210 single areas, is the greatest red wine producer. 40% of all German red wines come from the scattered vineyards between Bad Mergentheim in the north and Tübingen in the south. Annual mild temperatures, which are good for red vines, exist in the valley areas of the Neckar and the inflows of the Rems, Murr, Enz, Bottwar und Zaber rivers. These are protected by the Schwarzwald and Schwäbische Alb. The variety of red wines is worth mentioning: the classic Spätburgunder and Portugieser make up only a 3% share of the total cultivated area. The high quality wine is, as usual, Trollinger, a typical region Zechwine. The late maturing type of vine makes up only 22% of the annual wine quantity. Schwarzriesling comes second and these wines are usually mild and juicy. Lemberger, which produces heavy, full-bodied, fine herbal wines, is currently cultivated in an area of 2,500 acres. One can also find other types of wine in Württemberg such as Samtrot, Clevner, Muskattrollinger, Dornfelder, Helfensteiner,

Herold and Schillerwein, which is actually Rotling and is also blended from red grapes or mixtures.

Württemberg is the only German wine cultivation area where blending types is not taboo. On the contrary, there are even blends of red and white wine. Conditioned by the high share of red sorts, Barrique cultivation has become popular and has spread among the winegrowers since the middle of the 1980s. In Taubertal and in the area of Kocher-Jagst-Tauber, white wines are mostly grown in the Muschelkalk soils: Müller-Thurgau, Silvaner and Kerner. Nevertheless, Riesling (the Swabian wine) remains number one with a share of about 25% in an area of 6,700 acres.

The winemaking center lies between Heilbronn and the capitol of Stuttgart, in the lowlands of Württemberg. Here, in an area of 17,000 acres of fertile Trias and Muschelkalk soils, you can also find a great number of Riesling vines as well as Schwabian casual wines and high quality Lemberger and Spätburgunder. The wines from the valley of the Neckar are known for their slightly earthly taste. On the other hand, in the basin of Heilbronn and in the adjacent valleys, there are slimmer, more elegant wines. In the area of Stuttgart, vines grow among the houses and shops. There are juicy and full-bodied Trollinger wines, but also high

PECULIARITIES

Rotling/Schillerwein/Badisch Rotgold are created by the mixture of white wines and red grapes or of their must, which have to be pressed together. Rosé wine is Rotling from Württemberg, Badisch Rotgold is Rotling from Baden, which is created by mixing Grauburgunder and Spätburgunder vine types.

quality wines from Riesling grapes, Kerner and probably Silvaner in the famous valley of the Rems, on the southern slopes.

BADEN

The cultivated area in Southern Germany is the only wine region belonging to Wine Zone B. For Baden wine-growers, that means higher outputs of must weights to quality, degree and low enrichment quantities. The north-south area of the Baden vine slopes between Wertheim am Main in Baden Frankenland/Tauberfranken and Immenstaad am Bodensee is 250 miles. Over that distance, the climate and soil change make the wine offered particularly varied.

With a cultivation area of almost 4,000 acres, Baden is consequently the third largest cultivated area and is divided into eight areas, with 16 large and 324 single areas. The most renowned is Kaiserstuhl, the warmest corner of Germany, with about 11,000 acres of vineyards.

Until 1991, the present independent area of Tuniberg belonged to the area of Kaiserstuhl.

A mild climate, with the longest period of sunshine in Germany and volcanic soil, gives the wines of Kaiserstuhl a great deal of sophistication and elegance. Among Kaiserstuhl wines are Spätburgunder, Grauburgunder, Ruländer, Müller-Thurgau, Riesling and Silvaner. The most southern and simultaneously the highest above sea level of German vineyards are situated in the sub-glacial moraine soils am Bodensee. The classic Bodensee wine is Spätburgunder Weissherbst, but more grapes from Burgundy are fermented for elegant red wines. In the area of Markgräfler, between Südschwarzwald and Rhein, the vine area amounts to about 7,400 acres. The vineyards are located on the southern and western slopes in heavy loess and clay soils with various types of weathered limestone and marl. Here, an old culture vine is grown, mostly Gutedel, from which young wines are light and sharp. In Breisgau between Freiburg and Lahr, the vine slopes are situated in the sunny Schwarzwald-Vorbergen. Ruländer und Spätburgunder Weissherbste determine the wine panorama in the area of 5,000 acres.

In Ortenau, where Riesling and Spätburgunder are grown almost exclusively, a complete range of quality exists nearly every year, including Eiswines. It was not until the year 1996, that the area of Kraichgau was established, stretching from Rastatt to the north of Wiesloch. Müller-Thurgau, Riesling, Weiss- and Grauburgunder are the dominant vine types. The best wines grow on the loess slopes and have a special full-bodied and classy taste. Badische Bergstrasse (1,000 acres) is chiefly known for its classy Rieslings, which grow on the steep slopes with weathered soil and prehistoric rock.

The area of Tauberfranken is the coldest cultivated area of Baden. Vines are planted only on the Muschelkalk southern and southwestern slopes. Müller-Thurgau takes up half of the vine area. In Baden, there are about 120 winegrower's organizations, of which the Baden wine cellar in Breisach is the largest. Around 8000 winegrowers supply the largest German cellars with their grapes. In addition to the organizations, which secure the survival of small winegrowers, there are also young, developing family companies, which, through their assiduous and dedicated work, have catapulted the wines of Baden to the top.

SAALE-UNSTRUT

To be called "rosé," a wine must contain no less than 95% of a single red wine type.

The cultivated area of Saale-Unstrut lies to the south of the town of Halle in the state of Sachsen-Anhalt. 1000 years ago, the Cistercians planted the first grapes in the northern cultivated area of Europe. The present small area of about 1,200 acres lies beyond the 51st degree of latitude, which is regarded as the climatic border of world wine cultivation. The vine slopes near Eisleben are situated in the same altitude as the Ruhr area and even the Polish and English vineyards lie geographically further to the south than the cultivated area of Saale-Unstrut. The cultivated area, divided into two parts, four large areas and 18 single areas, confines itself to the wind protected areas on the southeast and southwest slopes in the narrow river valleys. Moreover, cultivation is favored by the microclimatic advantages and also by the geological structure of the countryside, which is chiefly constituted of Muschelkalk and new red sandstone soils. In the winemaking area near Unstrut, Freiberg, the largest cellars since can be found. At present, the winegrowers' organization of Freiberg has about 700 members, who work more than half of the vines in the winemaking area.

Since you can only count on a growing period of 190 days annually, on average, most winegrowers prefer premature types of grapes in the area of Saale and Unstrut: Müller-Thurgau is the main sort. These classy wines have a distinct character. In addition, Weissburgunder, Silvaner, Gutedel, Riesling, Kerner, Morio-Muskat and Bacchus are grown. Despite the few sunny hours, you come across red wines from Portugieser, Dornfelder and Spätburgunder grapes in the area of Saale and Unstrut, which can develop a strong sharpness. Meanwhile, in the case of reds, the winegrowers also risk Barrique cultivation. To the cultivated area belong the vineyards in Höhnstedt, Langenbogen, Seeburg and Rollsdorf, situated on the so-called "sweet lake" near Eisleben. Here, Traminer and Weissburgunder grow in slate soils. Conditioned by a high risk of frost, there are seldom late vintages in the entire winegrowing area. Yet, even without these quality grades, the small number of winegrowers in the area of Saale and Unstrut are almost always sold out.

Sachsen

Sachsen is the smallest and most eastern of all German winegrowing areas; it covers only 740 acres in four large and 17 single areas. Nevertheless, about 1500 winegrowers, mostly organized into the Sachsian winegrowers' organization, work there. The wines grow on the steep shores of the Elbe River Valley, between Dresden and Meissen. The weather is determined by continental influences: the summers are dry and hot and the winters are harsh and cold. Because of the climate, the grapes thrive only in a few places on the southern slant of the slope,

where the cold air flows off. In the area near Meissen, the terroir is defined by weathered granite. Between Radebeul and Dresden, it is primarily made up of weathered gneiss. Some small parts of the soil contain lime, clay, loess, sand and porphyry. Small grape terraces are typical of this type of winemaking, laboriously cultivated by hand. The yields of the vintage are therefore very low, on average 925 gallons per 2.5 acres.

There are four main types in the cultivated area of Sachsen: Müller-Thurgau, Riesling, Weissburgunder and Kerner. In addition, there are Traminer, Ruländer, Scheurebe and some new variants expected to bring high yields. The red wines play a subordinate role near the Elbe and are rare. Without exception, the wines from the area of the Elbe are light and can develop an extraordinary bouquet, although they are usually grown dry. Riesling wines are classy, Ruländer vintages are full-bodied and Müller-Thurgau wines posses certain elegance and delicacy. A peculiarity of this area is Goldriesling, a blend of Riesling and Courtillier Musqué, not cultivated in the old federal states.

Austria

Although wines from Austria only comprise 1% of worldwide wine production, the wines of the alpine republic are ranked among the best in Europe. As early as 3000 years ago, the Celts discovered the potential of the soil and the convenient climate conditions for growing wine in the area. The first boom of the Austrian winegrowing business was not noticed until the Middle Ages. Following the dénouement of the wine scandal in the middle of the 1980s, Austrian wines regained their international status by applying an assiduous quality policy.

The present wine cultivating area of Austria amounts to 12,000 acres. The wine areas are mainly situated in the east of the republic. Niederösterreich has the greatest share in vine areas with about 60%, followed by Burgenland with 34% and Steiermark with 6%.

WACHAU

The most famous wine region of Austria covers a vine area of about 4,000 acres and is cultivated by almost 1000 winegrowers. The countryside along its terraced, steep slopes near the Danube cannot be cultivated on a large scale using machines, thus necessitating laborious manual labor. In the juicy but infertile prehistoric rock, versatile, elegant, green Veltliner wines are grown, as well as Müller-Thurgau, Riesling, Zweigelt, St. Laurent and Blauer Portugieser. The grapes of green Veltliner and Riesling vines produce top international wines.

KREMSTAL

The wine area of Kremstal covers a cultivated area of about 62,000 acres around the town of Krems, stretching directly to Wachau. In the prehistoric rock and loess soils, green Veltliner wines are chiefly grown. More and more wine-growers of Kremstal opt for international types of vines, such as Chardonnay. A peculiarity of the area of Kremstal is the temperature fluctuation between day and night, which has a positive affect on the maturity of grapes. The warm climate from the East meets the cold climate of the West, and the wines flaunt their fully mature, juicy flavors.

KAMPTAL

The largest wine town of Langenlois lies in the center of the winegrowing area of 104,000 acres, where 90% of the white wine grapes are cultivated. The famous location of Kamptal is Heiligenstein near Zöbing, a name which goes back to a document from the year 1280. Even today, the southern slopes of a mountain called Höllenstein are home to the warmest vineyards in Austria. The weathered desert sandstone of the exposed wine locations, which comes from the distant past, provides good conditions to grow mainly green Veltliner and Riesling and produces strong, sharp, classy wines.

DONAULAND

The cultivated area is divided into three areas: Wagram, Klosterneuburg and Tulbing. Along the Wagram River, green Veltliner wines have a lion's share, about 65%, of this cultivated area. Weissburgunder and Riesling wines are also grown there. The wines from Klosterneuburg owe their classy, juicy character to the loess, clay and sandy subsoil. The institute for wine research and cultivation of fruits called "Höhere Bundeslehr- und Versuchsanstalt für Wein- und Obstzucht" has existed in Klosterneuburg for more than 150 years. Zweigelgrapes were cultivated in the area. In the wine area of Tulbing, the winegrowers specialize chiefly in the cultivation of green Veltliner wines.

Grüner Veltliner is Austria's most famous type of vine. All Austrian quality and high quality wines have a redwhite seal with the state control number on the neck of the bottle.

WEINVIERTEL

Weinviertel, also known as "Veltlinerland," is the largest Austrian cultivated area, with about 45,000 acres of vineyards.

This wine region is also known for its Welschriesling and these grapes are extensively used in the domestic production of sparkling wines. In Weinviertel, almost all types of vines are permitted; many winemaking estates combine winemaking with classic agriculture. Red wines are mainly grown in the region of Haugsdorf, but green Veltliner is the most common type of vine in Weinviertel.

THERMENREGION

Thermenregion, a small, but fine area, stretches 7,400 acres and is the warmest, driest cultivated area in Austria. Red wines, comprising 25% of the cultivated area, thrive in this climate. The vegetation phase is very long, extending through September to October. The soil characteristic ranges from a rocky, infertile subsoil to heavy and clay soils, favoring a variety of wines. The centers of red and quality wines are Bad Vöslau, Sooss and Baden not far from Vienna.

NEUSIEDLERSEE

In the north of Neusiedlersee, vineyards cover almost 27,000 acres of loess, black earth, gravel and sand. In good years, internationally renowned wines are grown. Neusiedlersee wines are full-bodied, elegant and distinct. The rich, full-bodied sweet wines belong to the list of top international wines due to the immense water vaporization of the lake and noble rot in the fall.

BURGENLAND

To the south of Neusiedlersee, the grapes benefit from the warmth coming from the Hungarian lowland. Middle Burgenland is one of few Austrian areas where mostly red wines are grown. Blaufränkisch vines particularly find ideal cultivation conditions in the deep, heavy soil, which produces strong, rich wines. South Burgenland is the smallest Austrian wine region with a cultivated area of about 1,140 acres. Almost half of the wines produced here are white wines. A regional specialty is a wine called Uhudler, from an old representative, which is not grafted according to the enrichment documents.

STEIERMARK

In the hilly area of south Steiermark, the wine area is concentrated only in a few centers along the southern Austrian slopes of Weinstrasse, Thermenland-Weinstrasse,

Oststeirischen Römerweinstrasse and Klöcher Weinstrasse. A peculiarity of the cultivated area lies in the volcanic soils, which give the wines a special mineral flavor. South Steiermark is mostly a region of juicy white wines. In contrast, western Steiermark is mainly known for Schilcher, a sharp rosé wine from the Blau Wildbacher grape.

VIENNA

Vienna and wine, they are two inseparable terms. The Roman legionnaires planted the first grapes here in the third century AD. At present, most of the vineyards are situated beyond the state border, on the shores of the Danube and at the foot of Bisamberg. To the south of Vienna, there are only a few places with a wine cultivation business. The wine of the current vintage can be sold from October 11th until the end of the coming year.

France

France has a total area of 2,500,000 acres, which are divided into 300 cultivated areas.

No other country in the world has fine wine so firmly engrained in its culture. French wines have been the top wines for centuries. The vineyards of Burgundy and Bordeaux have set the standards of the international wine world and have epitomized quality wine. Even though the price policy of the French top winegrowing estates still incurs a lot of criticism, it should not be forgotten that the top segment of French wines does not make up even 5% of the total wine quantity and cheaper, excellent wines are also produced.

Bordeaux

The region of Bordeaux has perfected every aspect of winemaking. Every sixth inhabitant of the old harbor town works directly or indirectly in the wine business. The first vineyard, Château, was established in 1550, in order to create a proper architectural setting for high quality wines. At present, there are about 10,000 Châteaux in a cultivated area of about 272,000 acres with their own wine names, not to mention simple brands. The most famous Bordeaux is Cabernet Sauvignon from the region of Médoc

and Graves, which makes up to 70% of the vine sort selection. The legendary red wine qualification was introduced in 1855 and was only adapted in the year 1973.

BURGUNDY

Benedict monks of the Cluny monastery and the Cistercians of the abbey of Clos de Vougeot decisively propagated Burgundy wine cultivation. The Cistercians discovered the impact of the terroir on the wines and divided their vine gardens into different areas, which were called Crus. At present, 8000 winegrowing estates cultivate a total area of about 56,000 to 116,000 acres in the area of Beaujolais.

The typification in Burgundy is divided according to AOC (Appellation d'Origine Contrôlée), Premiers Crus and Grands Crus. The main types of vine are Pinot Noir and in the Beaujolais area, Gamay dominantes.

CHAMPAGNE

It was not until 1927, that the region, which is referred to as Champagne, was exactly defined. It stretches from

Charly to the south of Paris, up to Reims and southwards over Epernay to Côte des Blancs. Its southern offsets are Côte de Sézanne. Traditionally, champagne is created from wines from different locations within the appellation and from the Pinot Noir, Pinot Meinier and Chardonnay grapes. In the blends of some great champagne estates, wines from up to 200 municipalities can be found.

Languedoc-Roussillon

Between the lake and the mountain ridges lies the highest French wine region, whose grapes grow on artifically built, narrow, steep terraces. For a long time, winegrowers exclusively mass-produced wines in the area of Languedoc-Roussillon, one of the largest homogenous cultivated areas in the world. But quality wine cultivation has slowly been adapted. Apart from the traditionally grown types of vines, such as Grenache, Carignan, Cinsault and Mourvèdre, international sorts still prevail in the vineyards of the area of Languedoc-Roussillon. In particular, Syrah, which produces juicy, full-bodied wines, has gained fame in recent years.

Alsace

The riotous political situation of Alsace mirrors its winemaking history. It was only after the Second World War, that the relatively cold climatic winemaking area of Alsace, found a new identity and a new quality policy for growing wine. In contrast with the rest of French wine regions, the types of vine are recorded on the label in Alsace. Despite an increase in the varieties, seven white types of vine represent classic Alsace wine tradition: Riesling, Gewürztraminer, Silvaner, Pinot Blanc, Pinot Gris, Muscat and Pinot Noir.

While Cuvées determine the wine stage in the southern cultivated areas, most wines from the northern regions are pressed from a single type of vine.

LOIRE

The Loire River, one of the last, wild, unstoppable watercourses in Europe, leaves its mark on the wine region, generating fresh, juicy red and white wines, along with rich, sweet wines. Chenin Blanc is a dominant type of grape, grown since the 9th century. The young wines smell of apple and citrus fruits and develop a distinct, aromatic taste with increasing age. Sauvignon Blanc is the most important wine cultivated in the area of Pouilly-Fumé and Sancerre, but also given a less known title of Menetou-Salon, Quincy and Reuilly. The classic red wine of the Loire River is Cabernet Franc.

RHÔNE

From the valley of the Rhône, comes a series of excellent, sweeter, drier, red, white and rosé wines. All share a distinctive, sharp taste. Famous appellations such as Hermitage, Gigondas and Châteauneuf-du-Pape, have made this wine region famous throught the world. These areas produce mostly red wines and small quantities of white wines. The classic red wines from Hermitage, with the smoky Brombera flavor, come exclusively from the Syrah grape. Among wines smelling of pepper, from which come the appellations of Châteauneuf-du-Pape and Gigondas and Syrah, there is also Grenache.

Italy

The Italian wine palette is as extensive and varied in quality as the land and its people. It is impossible to cover all the wines and vineyards of Italy. No other country has so much versatility in regard to type of vine, soil, and wine cultivation area as Italy, Sicily and Sardinia. The simplest country wines from the south are often produced from the regional types of vine and are mostly poured into big, one quart bottles. These belong to the Italian countryside wine tradition as do high quality wines from Toscana or Piemont, which have achieved top

The cultivated area of Italy amounts to about 2,224,000 acres. No other country in the world has such varied soils, microclimates and vine growing systems as Italy. The relatively chilly wine regions of Südtirol in the north of Italy are located about 1,200 miles from the volcanic soil of the winegrowing island Pantelleria.

prizes on the international wine market. Italian wines have something to say about life, and drinking pleasure and *la dolce vita.*

PIEMONT

The Greeks and Romans were the first winegrowers in the traditional area of Piemont, but the biggest boom came only two decades ago. Following the rise of Barolo, a wine from the Nebbiolo grape, Angelo Gaja, astonished the professional world by its Barrique-cask produced Barbaresco.

The pure Nebbiolo wines are still the top products from the area of Piemont, although the Barbera type of vine is the most grown grape in the area. Barbera wines are juicy and classy by nature. From the Dolcetto grape, the winegrowers of Piemont press mostly simple, light wines, which ideally suit the local cuisine.

SÜDTIROL AND TRENTINO

These two provinces lie between the crest of the Alps and the Gardasee and benefit particularly from the sunny climate of the region. Although Südtirol is known for simple red wines, elegant white wines have shifted to the top of the wine stage, especially Gewürztraminer with its aro-

matic, flowery bouquet, along with fresh, juicy Pinot Bianco. In the area of Trentino, the vines grow mostly in the valleys of Etsch, Valle Laghi and Val di Cembra. Chardonnay takes up a large share of the total cultivated area. Trentino has two other types of red wine: Marzemino and Teroldego, cultivated nowhere else in the world.

VENETO

From the edge of the Dolomites up to Poebene, the rich facets of the wine area of Veneto contain a variety of local vines whose diversity echoes the varied climates and soil conditions. Of all Venetian red and white wines, Prosecco is the most famous, ranked among the export hits of the region. The vine type Corvina produces grapes for the famous red wines of Veneto: Valpolicella Classico and Amarone della Valpolicella. In particular, the delicate fruit has made the regional grape the most important in Italy. The most grown white wine type is Garganega, which shows its best side in Soave Classico.

LOMBARDY

Lombardy is ranked among the most significant winemaking regions in Italy and lies in the middle of the Alp bend in an area affected by various microclimates. Wine growing is concentrated in the areas of Oltrepò Pavese, Franciacorta and Veltlin, with their high vine terraces. From the west shore of Gardasee come strong red wines, such as Rondinella, Merlot and Cabernet. White wines from Trebbiano Toscano, Garganega and local types of vine are pressed here. The wine region of Lugana became famous internationally for its "Vini da tavola."

FRIAUL

This renowned wine region owes its worldwide reputation to its modern white wines. The important cultivated area stretches along the Slovenian border and covers the DOC-regions Collio Goriziano in the south and Colli Orientali del Friuli in the province of Udine. In the middle of the region, the broad alluvial land stretches to the DOC-region of Friuli Grave which continues to the cultivated area of Piave and Lison-Pramaggiore in the neighboring vicinity of Veneto. Red vines find ideal growth conditions in the fertile soils. Merlot and Cabernet Franc are native to the area.

TOSCANA

Even though Toscana presents a relatively small cultivated area, it remains in the forefront of the production of high quality wines. Around 45% of the wines have the DOC or DOCG status, known under such names as

Brunello di Montalcino, Carmignano, Chianti, Chianti Classico, Vernaccia di San Gimignano and Vino Nobile di Montepulciano. Superb Toskaner wines classified as "Vini da tavola" belong to the high quality wines on the international wine stage today. Cabernet Sauvignon and Merlot still prevail in the local vineyards. They are often blended with Sangiovese or aged in the Barrique cask.

Sardinia

Just in the past few years, the wines from this Mediterranean island have established quality and won prestige. Progress has been made through the commitment of private and organizational cellars and they are staying ahead of other wine regions of Italy. White wines have a great share of the wine production. Particularly in the west of the island, two very special white wines are produced: the dry Vernaccia di Oristano wines with a high alcohol content, and the rare Malvasia di Bosa wines, which are similar to non-spiked sherry. In the northern part of the island, sweet, fine and aromatic white wines come from DOC Moscato di Sorso-Sennori.

SICILY

The largest Mediterranean island belongs among the oldest European winemaking regions. The island was known for its anonymous, mass-produced wines for a long time. However, the last few years have shown an increasing consciousness of quality in Sicily. 75% of Sicilian wine production is comprised of white wine. The most important wine province is Messina in the east where the red Faro is pressed from Nerello Mascalese and Nerello Cappuccio. The most representative DOC wine from the southeast of Sicily is called Cerasuolo di Vittoria. It is a mild, highly alcoholic wine, which harmonizes with the regional cuisine.

Spain

According to the size of its vine area, Spain is the largest wine country in the world, but it is behind Italy and France in the quantity of wine produced, a statistic which can be ascribed to the seasonal drought that keeps grape yields low in most of the country. It was only a few years ago that modern and quality-oriented wine cultivation penetrated into traditional Spanish agriculture. The most renowned Spanish wine region, Rioja, produces high quality wines, but smaller and less cultivated areas of the Iberian Peninsula

Spain, with about 3,000,000 acres, has the largest cultivated area in the world; however, the annual yield quantity is behind Italy and France, which holds third place in world production.

have immensely improved the quality of their wines as well.

RIOJA

The most famous cultivated area of Spain lies on the fertile river shores of the Ebro. Sharp and rich red wines, which have shown their mature potential for many years, have made the region famous. Rioja is composed of two sub-zones: Rioja Alta, with its vine slopes in the rising hills, and Rioja Baja, the warmest and driest region. The typical Rioja wine consists of 80% Tempranillo and there are small quantities of Garnacha and Cariñena grapes. The famous wine is also partly blended with Cabernet Sauvignon and Merlot.

PRIORATO

The small but fine wine region of Priorato, covers all nine wine countries in the hilly hinterland of Tarragona. Originally, only Cariñena grapes were grown there, and only at the end of the 1980s, when the traditional Garnacha grape experienced a renaissance, did Cabernet Sauvignon become popular in a few vineyards. The full-bodied red wines have a great maturation potential and are famous for their longevity.

Penedés

Cava, a Spanish sparkling wine, is produced according to the traditional bottle-fermentation method and has made the wine regions to the south of Barcelona famous. Cava, which is produced from the grape-sorts Macabeo, Xarel-lo and Parellada, usually must stay in yeast for at least nine months – Cava vintages for even four years. Apart from the sparkling wine production, succulent white wines come from the wine regions, which draw substances from the cretaceous clay soils of Penedés. The red wines are pressed from the Cariñena, Garnacha and Monastrell sorts.

Ribera del Duero

The vineyards of this region are situated along the shores of the Duero River, which has experienced a comet-like rise in the past years. The vicinity has climatic contradictions: long, frosty-cold winters are followed by short, dry summers. The Tempranillo vine, also called Tinto Fino or Tinto del País, is grown here. The most famous winegrowing estate is "Bodegas Vega Sicilia." From this area, strong, structurally rich and elegant red wines are blended with Cabernet Sauvignon, Merlot and Malbec.

Portugal

The smallest country in the western part of the Iberian Peninsula was woken from its drunken slumber only a few years ago. That is to say, Port wine has been an export hit since the 17th century, but traditional wine was the main business. At present, the young winegrowers' generation is trying to reap the enormous potential of the climate and soils to produce wines which are not overshadowed by their great Spanish competitors. In the cold, northern Atlantic climate, full-bodied wines now grow and a renaissance of the Portuguese wine business has begun.

The cultivated area of Portugal is 618,000 acres. Portugal is regarded as the country of 500 types of vine and so posesses the largest variety of types of vine in the world. Most of the wines are traditionally produced from many types of vine.

VINHO VERDE

The area of Verde in the north of Portugal is simultaneously the largest DOC-region in the country. The "green wine," which makes up the largest share of the Portuguese wine production, comes in two versions: first, there are red, tannin bitter wines, largely drunk in the country, followed by white wines, including Port, Portugal's most important export wine. Lighter, carbonic acid gas wines containing some residual sugar have a succulent flavor. Earlier, Vinho always underwent malolactic fermentation, which produces carbonic-acid gases. Currently, carbonic-acid gases are added to the in-

dustrial wine Vinho Verde, which makes up 90% of production. The wine is pressed from entirely different types of vine, mostly from blends of regional grapes. The best sort is Alvarinho, which is grown in the north, on the border with Gaul.

Douro

The classic cultivated area of Port wine, named after the port from which it is shipped, lies to the east of Porto am Oberlauf off the Douro-River. The vine terraces are situated in the weathered slate soils which stretch all the way to the hinterland. The soils store moisture so that the sensitive vines are supplied with sufficient water during the summer drought. In Douro, Portugal's best red wine, Barca Velha, is grown.

ALENTEJO

A great number of fashionable wines come from Alentejo, enabling the area to gain a position among internationally recognized vineyards.

Fine, structured white wines and strong red wines with full, mature flavors are produced from vines grown in hot soils where in summers the temperatures are usually 104°F. When speaking of vines, one must mention the Aragonez grape which gives elegance and structure to the wines. The terroir consists mostly of slate, granite and quartzite with parts of marble taken from the earth in the area of Esrtemoz and Borba.

South Africa

The wine-growing region of South Africa dates back to the year 1652, when the first Europeans stepped onto South African soil. Today, the total cultivated area amounts to 300,000 acres and it is increasing. Since the end of Apartheid, winemaking on the Cape has experienced a rise. Wines from Stellenbosch or Paarl are sought after as never before, and the cultivated area of the red types of wine such as Cabernet Sauvignon, Merlot, Shiraz and Pinotage is increasing enormously. International white types of wine such as Chardonnay and Sauvignon Blanc prevail in the Cape vineyards. These wines are grown both in vats and in wooden casks, particularly in the cold, coastal regions. Despite the heat, many South African wines have more sharpness than expected because this area lies mainly in the cold flows from Antarctica. The winds cool off in the cold flow and provide an appropriate wine-growing climate on the Cape.

The cultivated area in South Africa amounts to about 300,000 acres. About 80% is planted with white types of vine.

Chile

Chile has almost a Mediterranean climate. Winemaking has been practiced in Chile for more than 400 years. The Spaniards planted the first vines, and thus the oldest wine country of the Southern Hemisphere came into existence. However, Chilean wine production opened up to the international market only in the past few years. Since the middle of the 19th century, Cabernet Sauvignon, Merlot, Chardonnay and Sauvignon Blanc have been cultivated. Presently, Chardonnay presents the most

significant growth and is mainly aged in the small Barrique-casks. As for red wines, Cabernet Sauvignon comes second and especially in the warmer regions, this type of vine finds ideal growth conditions. Cassis gives a typical touch. A eucalyptus flavor often comes out in Chilean Cabernet, and emphasizes its succulent taste.

The cultivated area of Chile amounts to 20,000 acres, and is increasing. About 60% of the vicinity is planted with red types of vine.

The United States: California

In the past decades, the winemaking business has gone through an unprecedented boom on the west coast of North America. Today, on the coastland between Seattle, in Washington State and Los Angeles, California, Chardonnay, Cabernet Sauvignon, Sauvignon Blanc, Pinot Noir, Merlot and Syrah vines are grown, making California the nation's wine country. Proximity to the ocean, morning fog and cold winds create ideal growth conditions for wine in the hot wine region, in particular in the Napa and Sonoma Valleys. The vine area covers 930,000 acres; the wine quantity produced amounts to almost 90% of the total wine production in the United States. Besides legendary vineyards such as Mondavi, Gallo, Simi and Fetzer, 900 new winemaking estates have been established.

Australia

Australia is the first country of the New World, whose top wines were introduced to the international markets. An Australian peculiarity is to blend two or more wine types.

At the beginning of the 20th century, sherry and Madeira wine styles were in demand in Australia and a more significant sales market was developing in Great Britain. Since the 1950s, Australian winegrowers have concentrated on the cultivation of dry wines. At present, around 1100 estates cultivate a vine area of 371,000 acres. Chardonnay is the most common type of white vine and the wines range from light wines with fresh citrus aromas to heavy, valuable wines, which come from the warm cultivated areas. The Australian red wine stage is dominated by the Shiraz grape, which produces succulent wines with a sharp flavor. The largest wine companies have their seat in Australia in the following areas: Barossa Valley, Clare Valley, McLaren Valley, Coonawarra and Padthaway.

New Zealand

Between the 38th and 45th degrees of latitude, winegrowing is carried out in New Zealand. The country has the southernmost wine regions in the Southern Hemisphere at its disposal. The influence of the Pacific, in particular its strong west winds and abundant showers, provide a relatively cold climate. Only 30 years ago, the Montana Company risked the colder climate of the southern island. Previously, winegrowing was exclusively run on the northern island. The total winegrowing area is only about 30,000 acres, cultivated by about 350 winegrowing estates. Chardonnay and Sauvignon Blanc are the dominant wines on both islands and most wines are aged in the Barrique. A specialty of New Zealand's production is Sauvignon Blanc, which primarily enchants the taster with its intensive flavors of gooseberry, passion fruit, lemons and green asparagus. The wines of New Zealand are chiefly pressed from the Pinot Noir grape.

The most important types of vine are Chardonnay, Sauvignon Blanc, Müller-Thurgau, Riesling, Chenin Blanc, Pinot Noir, Merlot, Cabernet Sauvignon and Shiraz. The most famous regions: Auckland, Hawkes Bay, Cloudy Bay and Marlborough.

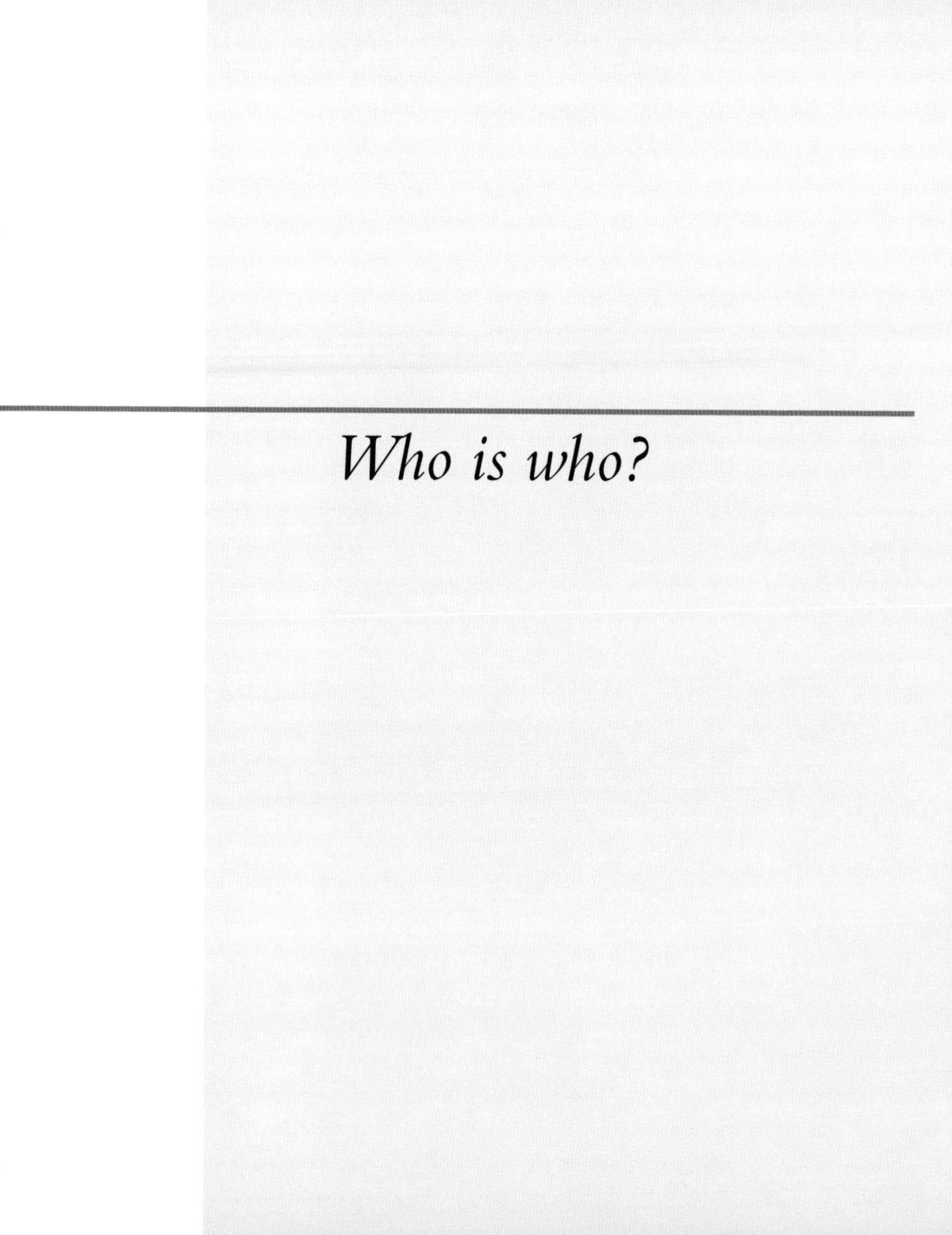

Who is who?

PETRUS

Who is who?

INSTRUCTIONS AND LABELS :

The language of the labels has become complex: are we dealing here with company names, brand names, the type of vine, a fantasy name or a place of origin? In truth, the label is the signboard of the wine and naturally a sales promoting marketing weapon in the ruthlessly competitive wine market. The labels of the famous winemaking estates have renowned symbols or colors. The tower of Château Latour or the sky-blue label of the Robert Weil estate send an evocative message to the customer; a signal of significant effect independent of the information on the label.

What must be stated on a German label is precisely regulated by the Wine Act. The following names are stipulated: the name of the cultivated area, the vintage, the name of the producer, the term of the filling or the name of the winegrower's filling – in contrast to the filling in the cellar. More and more winegrowers give the facts of the place and area names and they state the type of vine and the corresponding quality degree on the label. These are in ascending sequence: table wines, quality wines of the specific winegrowing area (QbA), high quality white wines, late vintage, high quality wines made from selected grapes and high quality wines made from selected grapes (BA), wines made from choice grapes left on the vine to dry out at the end of the season (TBA) and Eiswines. The facts concerning the filling quantity are obligatory, along with the alcohol content and the authorized control number, where both last numbers refer to the year of the bottle filling. It is often the case that a logo or label of the winegrowing estate is placed on the back side of the label.

The same strict regulations are valid for Bordeaux wines. Besides the wine name or brand (Château), the following must be given: the qualification, the specification of origin, and the vintage, the name and address of the owner, the alcohol degree and the bottle content. Apart from the classifications of Crus (Premier Cru, Grand Cru), which are different in Bordelais and Burgundy, French wines are distinguished by the terms AC (Appellation Contrôlée for high quality wines from specific cultivated areas) and AOC (Appellation d'Origine Contrôlée for wines with an obvious origin and strict production regulations), which stand for controlled origin and quality tests. AC wines are the French counterparts to quality wine, as defined by EU law. The geographical determination forms the basis for the AC and brand and generic names are protected from misuse.

The same control system for quality wines exists in the Italian Wine Act, known under the term DOC (Denominazione di Origine Controllata). According to the DOC, the winegrow-

ing areas and names of the vine types, the minimum and maximum alcohol content, the total sharpness and extract content, yield limits and wine preparation practices are important. The quality name DOCG (Denominazione di Origine Controllata e Garantita) has been used since 1963 in Italy, and is meant to distinguish the high quality wines of the country.

The Spanish Wine Act covers regulations for production, name and wine sales. Moreover, it contains guidelines for the qualification, the quality category and the specification of origin, winegrowing and cellar techniques and the making of the bottle and the label. The top of the name pyramid is represented by DOCa-wines (Denominación de Origen Calificada). The grapes must come from a specific area and the permitted maximum yield is strictly stipulated and is lower than in all other qualifications. Additionally, DOCa-wines ensure that the types of vinegrowing and storing correspond to the legal regulations. Next, there are 54 permitted zones for DO-wines (Denominación de Origen), where less strict regulations apply. Wines with the geographical name of origin and a particular regional character are summarized in the classification Vino de la Tierra (VdlT). The name Vino Comarcal (VC or CV) determines wines chiefly produced with a regional character in the 21 classified areas. The lowest quality Spanish wines are table wines (Vino de Mesa – VdM). To ensure the quality of Crianza, the wines must prove maturity over a period of two years, at least six months of which are spent in a wooden cask. The areas of Rioja and Ribera del Duero even require twelve months. For the name Reserva, the wines must mature at least three years, with a year in wood or in the bottle. Gran reserva is a name used exclusively for wines which were aged for five years: two years in the wood cask and three years in the bottle.

Winegrowers overseas have less freedom as to the label information. In the United States, the following data is obligatory: the name of the producer, the type of wine, protected fantasy names, fillers (grown, produced and bottled or Estate bottled), the alcohol content, the content of sulfur, the misuse warning and the filling quantity.

Australian wines can either be classified as red wine (which must contain 80% of the specified sort) or as blends brought to the market; for the wines from New Zealand, the product names, the producer with the name and his address, along with the alcohol content and bottle content are stipulated.

The Wine Act in South Africa differentiates between "Non-certified wines," such as table wines commonly sold on the market, and "certified wines," which have the specification of origin (Wine of Origin) and the guarantee of the type of the vine, the vintage and origin.

In the EU, the wine hierarchy knows the quality level which all wines produced in Europe have to match: quality wines must have a specification of origin, which permits them to be on the market.

Similarly, one can also find the cultivated area, the name of the producer, the type of vine, the filling quantity of the bottle and the alcohol content on the South African label.

Which type of vine is hidden behind the wines?

You may feel helpless and ignorant when buying a wine: fantasy names, established brand names, famous labels, but no reference to the origin and the type of vine? So, what is hidden behind the names, commonly known to everyone else? Which vines are behind the great French, Italian and Spanish wines?

FRANCE

RED

BORDEAUX: Cabernet Sauvignon, Cabernet Franc

Graves (Bordeaux): Cabernet Sauvignon, Cabernet Franc, Merlot

SAINT-EMILION (BORDEAUX): Merlot, Cabernet Sauvignon, Cabernet Franc

BEAUJOLAIS BURGUNDY: Gamay, Pinot Noir, Pinot Gris, Chardonnay, Aligoté

CHÂTEAUNEUF-DU-PAPE (RHÔNE): Grenache Noir, Cinsault, Syrah

CÔTE RÔTIE (RHÔNE): Syrah

GIGONDAS (RHÔNE): Grenache Noir, Syrah

Bandol: Mourvèdre, Grenache, Cinsault

Hermitage: Syrah, Marsanne, Roussanne

The mixture relation of Cuvées is dependant on the producer, is different from year to year and cannot be actually specified. The order of the mentioned types of wine is showed by weighing the share of the respective type of vine in the wine.

WHITE

BORDEAUX SEC: Sémillion, Sauvignon Blanc

CHABLIS (BURGUNDY): Chardonnay

BOURGOGNE ALIGOTÉ: Aligoté, Chardonnay

SANCERRE (LOIRE): Sauvignon Blanc

Beaujolais (Burgundy): Chardonnay, Aligoté

CHAMPAGNER: Pinot Noir, Pinot Meunier, Chardonnay

Crémant d'Alsace: Riesling, Pinot Blanc, Pinot Noir, Pinot Gris, Auxerrois,

CHARDONNAY POUILLY-FUMÉ: Sauvignon Blanc

HERMITAGE: Marsanne, Roussanne

BANDOL: Bourboulenc, Clairette, Ugni Blanc

ITALY

RED

BARBARESCO (PIEMONT): Nebbiolo

BARBERA D'ASTI (PIEMONT): Barbera, Freisa, Grignolino

BAROLO (PIEMONT): Nebbiolo

CHIANTI (TOSCANA): Sangiovese, Canaiolo Nero, Trebbiano

SASSICAIA (TOSCANA): Cabernet Sauvignon

VINO NOBILE DI MONTEPULCIANO (TOSCANA): Sangiovese, Lanaiolo Nero

VALPOLICELLA (VENETIEN): Corvina Veronese, Rondinella, Molinara

WHITE

ASTI (PIEMONT): Moscato

PIEMONTE SPUMANTE: Chardonnay, Pinot Bianco, Pinot Grigio, Pinot Nero

SOAVE (VENETIEN): Garganega, Pinot Bianco, Chardonnay

ESTESTEST: Malvasia, Trebbiano

FRASCATI: Malvasia, Trebbiano, Greco

SPAIN

RED

CIGALES: Tempranillo, Garnacha

NAVARRA: Tempranillo, Garnacha Tinta, Cabernet Sauvignon, Merlot

PRIORATO: Garnacha Tinta, Garnacha Peluda, Cabernet Sauvignon

Rioja: Tempranillo, Garnacha, Cabernet Sauvignon

WHITE
CAVA: Xarel-lo, Parellada, Macabro, Chardonnay

GIANTS FOR THE TREMENDOUS THIRST

Collecting wine is an expensive and exclusive hobby, especially when it comes to large bottles. The large bottle trend began only at the beginning of the 1980s. Ten years later, following the boom of Bordeaux, it has intensified. German winegrowers have filled their top wines into large bottles, or, depending on the type of wine, into oversized vessels with capacity of up to six quarts.

Many wine collectors praise the perfect maturity of good wines. The smaller the bottle, the faster the wine matures. The development of a wine differs in various bottle sizes. The phenomenon can be observed especially with Bordeaux and Burgunder: quite a few winegrowing estates have already poured their excellent vintages into wine bottles between ½ and 18 quarts in size.

The Biblical naming of such special formats can be confusing and misleading. In the various French winegrowing areas, there are different names for the same bottle sizes:

BURGUND

Demi bouteille	0.375 quarts
Bouteille	0.75 quarts
Magnum	1.5 quarts
Jéroboam	3 quarts
Réhoboam	4.5 quarts
Méthusalem	6 quarts
Salmanazar	9 quarts
Balthazar	12 quarts
Nabuchodonosar	15 quarts

BORDEAUX

Demi bouteille	0.375 quarts
Bouteille	0.75 quarts
Magnum	1.5 quarts
Doppelmagnum	3 quarts
Jéroboam	4.5 or 5 quarts
Impériale	6 quarts
Salmanazar	9 quarts
Balthazar	12 quarts
Nabuchodonosar	15 quarts
Melchior	18 quarts

CHAMPAGNE

Quar	0.187 quarts
Demi bouteille	0.375 quarts
Demi-litre (outside the EU)	0.5 quarts

Bouteille	0.75 quarts
Magnum	1.5 quarts
Jéroboam	3 quarts
Méthusalem	6 quarts
Salmanazar	9 quarts
Balthazar	12 quarts
Nabuchodonosar	15 quarts

A STROLL THROUGH THE CLASSIFICATION OF WINE

The wine world needs more or less reliable constants to guarantee a certain quality of winegrowing and cultivation, transparent and imitable for everyone. That is the purpose of classifications, which specify minimal demands for the quality of grapes and a specific production and storing procedure. The soil itself, along with the area or plot in which the grapes grow, certainly can be reason for the quality and there has been some evidence of the uniqueness or performance efficiency of the terroir over the centuries.

Granted, the measures for classification are controversial, but they assure both consumers and winegrowers of the quality of the product. The classifications are also upheld by the winegrowers' manual mastery, for mass production does not provide a consistant indication of high quality. The most renowned classification models, which serve as an example for many other countries, come from France, and the most prominent one is from Bordelais.

CLASSIFICATION IN BORDELAIS

The first elaboration of the list of the winegrowing estates in Bordelais took place as early as the beginning of the 18th century.

The most significant Bordeaux classification has been opened for more than 100 years and it was adapted only once, in 1973. For that reason, certain Bordeaux arrangements have only a limited validity. On the other hand, the best and most expensive wines have no official classification.

On the occasion of the world exhibition in 1885, fifty-nine wines of Haut-Médoc and Haut-Brion from Graves, as well as 21 winegrowing estates from Sauternes, were officially selected in the ranking of Crus in total. The ranking was organized into five stages: from Premier to Cinquième Cru Classé. This classification was given exclusively to winegrowing estates which produced high quality wines for the longest period of time and which won the highest average prices. Cru Classé has been regarded as an historic winegrowing estate since 1932 and, correspondingly, is in high demand. For about 50 years, the Appellations Saint-Emilion (which is adapted every ten years) and Graves have recognized the official ranking. Fronsac, Pomerol

and the rest of the areas of Bordelais recognize the official classifications as well.

The classifications in Médoc:

Premiers Grands Crus Classés
Deuxième Grands Crus Classés
Troisième Grands Crus Classés
Quatrième Grands Crus Classés
Cinquième Grands Crus Classés
Crus Bourgeois
Cru Artisans
AOC Médoc

Crus Bourgeois

Médoc, an area in the middle of France, owes its name to its geographical location. The cultivated area with the famous appellations such as Margaux, Saint-Julien and Pauillac lies on the 45th degree of latitude between the Atlantic and the mouth of the Gironde River in southwest France. As in all French growing areas, the vineyards of Médoc are divided into forty different quality grades. The Médoc classification consists of sixty Crus Classés (since 1855), around 400 Crus Bourgeois, 300 Crus Artisans, other Crus and finally the wines growers' organization. The term "Crus Bourgeois" comes from the Middle Ages and was introduced as the official name for wines. The association "Crus Bourgeois du Médoc" supervises the observance of the specific regulations and production rules. So only the wines from the real Appellation of Médoc may be used for Crus Bourgeois. The winegrowing estates must posess at least seven hectares of cultivated area and the wines must be aged in their own cellars as well.

Crus Bourgeois makes up almost half of the wine production in Médoc –about 7500 hectares of vineyards and almost 55 million bottles. At present, you can find Crus Bourgeois and relatively good value Bordeaux wines in the category. Crus Bourgeois are usually pressed from the Cabernet-Sauvignon grape and can contain a high share of Merlot – mostly completed by Cabernet Franc. According to experience, the wines are ready to be drunk four to eight years after the vintage.

Currently, the Industrial and Commercial Chamber is working on the official classification. The wines are divided into three categories: Crus Bourgeois Exceptionnels, Crus Bourgeois Supérieurs and Crus Bourgeois. This new classification is opened to all wines of Médoc and is controlled and, if necessary, newly stipulated by an independent committee every ten years.

THE CLASSIFICATIONS OF GRAVES:

Premier Grand Cru Classé

Crus Classés Graves

AOC Graves

THE CLASSIFICATIONS IN SAINT-EMILION:

Premiers Grands Crus Classés A
Premiers Grands Crus Classés B
Grand Crus Classés
Grand Crus
AOC St.-Emilion

CLASSIFICATION IN BURGUNDY

The Burgundy quality pyramid and the corresponding designation system are now a guide to a variety of wines. Shortly after the establishment of INAO (Institute National des Appellations d'Origine) in 1935, more significant descriptions of origin were established in Burgundy. The established regional classifications, dating from the middle of the 19th century, were taken into account. The Burgundy quality hierarchy forms the regional and communal names up to Grand-Cru names. Today, the statutes of controlled descriptions of origin AOC cover the following factors: the types of vine, the traditional growing techniques, the minimum and maximum alcohol content as well as the region-typical wine characteristics.

The simplest regional AOC is Bourgogne. All white and red wines pressed from selected grapes in Burgundy are entitled to this description. AOC Bourgogne can be complemented by designations, connected with additional production.

Example: Bourgogne Aligoté must be pressed from a pure white wine grape. Red wine Bourgogne Passe-tout-grain may be pressed maximally from two thirds of Gamay and minimally one third of Pinot Noit.

Other ingredients demarcate the regional origin. More than 50% of all wines in Burgundy carry a regional AOC on the label.

The communal AOCs (Villages) stand for a typical characteristic connected with a specific wine-growing municipality. If the name of a single area is mentioned, then the respective wine must come from it.

AOC Grand Cru is exclusively reserved to 32 areas of Côte d'Or as well as seven areas of Chablis. For Grands Crus, strict yield limits per one hectare apply. Its share of the total quantity of all produced wines in Burgundy is barely 2%.

FIRST WINES FROM THE CLASSIFIED AREAS IN RHEINGAU

Since the vintage of 1999, wines from the officially classitied areas have been designated "first wines" for the first time.

About 2,718 acres of wine-cultivation area are defined on the winegrowing estate map as classified terroir – it roughly corresponds to one third of the total area of Rheingau. The area map, drawn up by the German weather service, regards not only the quality continuance of a vineyard area, but also the climatic conditions and the soil conditions in the vineyard. Further criteria are strict selection and the low hectare yield closely connected with it. A maximum of 50 hectoliters per hectare are permitted. The wine harvest, selective or by hand, is strictly stipulated.

Another prerequisite for receiving acclaim as a "first wine" is the sensory test. Experts examine the first wines thoroughly, assessing the color, the smell and the taste. They do not know, of course, which wines are from which winegrowers and they follow the rules of blind tasting strictly during the sensory examination. Rheingau, der Riesling and der Spätburgunder can be exclusively marketed as first wines. Additionally, there are dry grown wines and top Riesling and Spätburgunder. It is possible to recognize first wines at first sight by the three Romanesque arches on a black beam on the label. First wines may be offered no sooner than the 1st of September of the coming harvest year.

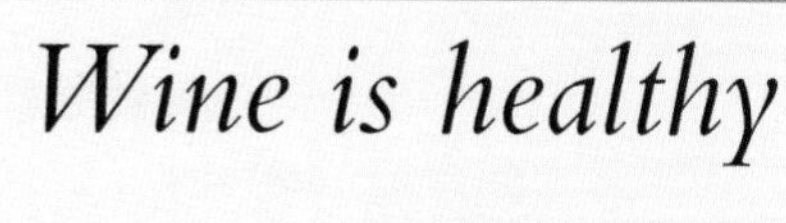

Wine is healthy

LB
8LJB

Wine is healthy

What makes wine healthy? Various astonishing factors act in harmony to make this drink really healthy. However, red and white wines do not differ only in their color.

As far as the total sharpness content is concerned, average red wines show, as opposed to white wines, lower values and are therefore more wholesome for stomach sensitive people. A red wine is richer in phenolic elements such as coloring substances, tannin, and phenolic carbon acids than the comparable white wine.

A red wine characteristic is the tannin-content. Red wines rich in tannin bring about slower and more lasting effects over a longer period of time than white wines. Red wines also contain fewer aromatic substances and, together with lower acid values and a higher drinking temperature, lead to a healthier stomach and intestines. Red wines are more relaxing and soporific than white wines, which tend to rouse and stimulate.

Higher doses of vitamins and trace elements usually come out in red wines compared to white wines.

The positive effects of a moderate wine treat include: higher spirits, improved digestion, healthy blood pressure and better coronary circulation. These effects have been proved in international studies. A pilot study found out as early as in 1996 that moderate wine consumption protects the heart. German doctors recommend that women should not more than 0.7 oz of alcohol and a man not more than 1 oz. For positive health effects, it is, however, important to drink wine regularly and not in broken intervals or in large quantities.

Most diabetics may enjoy wine. Wines, which have up to 0.7 oz of sugar, half of which is glucose, are permitted.
More detailed specifications are stated on the back label of the wine bottle.

ECO-WINES

Decades ago, concerned winegrowers started to work with conventional, well-tested methods in the vineyards and cellars. Ecology in the vineyard considers nature and allows sufficient time and space to produce healthy vines without chemical and genetic supplements. Eco winegrowers consciously give up fertilizers and use exclusively organic and mineral compost.

To work ecologically means to cultivate vines in harmony with nature, giving up chemicals and gene technologies and ensuring the protection of vitally important resources such as water and soil. In the end, the natural product is wine that offers authentic and unerring evidence of its growth circumstances in each glass. Ecological wine growing is inseparably connected with nature's obstacles and difficulties and a great number of winegrowers have proven that ecologically-produced top quality wines are possible and can delight the taste buds while leaving Nature intact.

Information about ecologically cultivated wines, also known as bio-winers, is available on the internet or in specialized stores selling biological products.

Champagne & Co.

Champagne & Co.

No other wine drink stands for festive occasions and tingling passions like Champagne. But only wine which comes from specific winegrowing regions and is produced according to strict rules may be called Champagne. The winegrowing area was exactly defined in 1927 and stretches from Charly, east of Paris, all the way to Reims, the capitol of Champagne. There is only one appellation for champagne. The best vineyards are situated on the slopes which are typical of the countryside. Here, the vine roots run deep into the cretaceous soil and offer the best conditions for the water balance of the vines.

Champagne is a blend produced from Pinot Noir, Pinot Meunier and Chardonnay. Traditionally, it is created from wines from different areas within the Appellation. Large champagne estates use wines from more than 200 municipalities for their products. Between 10 to 50% of older vintages are mixed with basic, new wines, which are stored in the stainless steel vats (assemblage).

Following the first fermentation, most basic wines undergo the malolactic fermentation (change of malic acid into milder lactic acid). The result is the so-called Vin Clair. Before it is poured into

About 80% of all champagnes come to the market without vintage specifications and are composed of many vintages. This procedure is called assemblage. For the production of champagne, 8,818 lbs of grapes but not more than 145.3 gallons of the must can be pressed.

the bottle, a mixture of wine, sugar and specially developed yeast are added: the so-called dosage (0.846 oz of sugar per quart). As soon as the bottles are closed with crown caps, yeast begins to ferment the sugar. After one or two months, the fermentation is finished.

The wine stays in yeast between nine months and five years, which keeps it fresh and gives it a distinctive yeasty taste. In the course of storing, the bottles are turned slightly every day, so that the yeast is loosened and the dead yeast sinks into the neck of the bottle. To remove the yeast, the bottle is frozen in an ice bath and when it is opened under pressure, carbonic acid shoots out like a cork from the bottle. Before the pure wine is closed again, the filling level, in which sugar syrup is dissolved, is evened out.

Sparkling wines

When producing sparkling wines, we can differentiate between two production procedures:

1. TRADITIONAL PROCEDURE/MÉTHODE CHAMPENOISE

According to the traditional or classical procedure, the second fermentation takes place in the bottle. Subsequently, individual bottles are shaken by hand or by a machine, while the yeast settles as a deposit in the neck of the bottle. Afterwards, it is removed without leaving the bottle. This procedure is demanding, relatively expensive and correspondingly noted on the bottle. If the sect is kept for a longer time in the yeast, then the procedure surpasses the quality guarantee of the end product and other production procedures.

2. THE TRANSVASIER-PROCEDURE OR FILTRATION YEAST REMOVAL

With this method, the demanding and expensive Degorier-procedure (yeast removal) is avoided. The wine is also fermented in the bottle and the bottles are emptied under retrogressive pressure into a vat and the yeast is filtered out. The note, "bottle fermentation," is allowed on the label of the bottle.

3. VAT FERMENTATION

In this case, the basic wine ferments in large, pressured vessels, enabling the production of larger and more homogenous batches. Following the fermentation process and the yeast removal by means of filtration, the sect is filled into the bottles. The procedure is cost-effective and is applied in the industrial production of sects and sparkling wines.

CRÉMANT

The term Crémant applies to all French sparkling wines produced outside Champagne after the European Union banned the use of the term, *Méthode champenoise.* No specific types of vine are designated for Crémant but there are fixed production conditions cited in all regions. Crémant may only be produced by means of the grape pressing procedure and the maximal yield from 330 lbs of grapes must not exceed 24.6 gallons. In addition, another law states that

the sugar content must be below 1.75 oz per quart. The name Crémant is also permitted in Germany.

The most significant French areas of origin for Crémant are determined by the production volumes of the following: Crémant d'Alsace, Crémant de Die, Crémant de Bourgogne, Crémant de Loire, Crémant de Limoux and Crémant de Bordeaux.

SECT

The origin of the term 'sect,' used for sparkling wines in German speaking countries since 1900, is not precisely defined. A sect can only be marketed as a German sect if it is made of 100% German wines. The same blend rules apply to wine. The blends from other areas are permitted, so that a German sect, provided it does not have any specific area specification, may come from vine types from other cultivated areas. The specification ("Sekt b.A." or "Qualitätsschaumwein b.A.") must be stated on the label along with the name of the cultivated area where

Sparkling wine is a wine with a carbon acid pressure of 1 to 2.5 bars. Carbon acid pressure is formed during fermentation or is achieved by additives of fermentation carbon acids before the wine preparation.

the grapes had been picked for production.

The most important quality feature of the sect is the basic wine. Proper sect production begins with the second fermentation, in which a small amount of sugar and yeast is added. Carbonic acid develops in the course of this process, is kept and represents one of decisive product features of the sparkling wine.

German sects only make up about 10% of the total production. German wine growers' sects enjoy a high reputation as very individual products, for example, high quality sect vines, produced in small amounts, manually and from one's own grapes. The winegrowers' sects must be produced according to the traditional bottle fermentation procedure and must indicate the vintage, the type of vine and the producer on the label.

SPUMANTE

Due to the Prosecco boom in the 1990s, Italian sparkling wines have become very popular. The most noted types of vine are Pinot in all its varieties. However, the most famous are Moscato grapes, from which aromatic Asti wines are pressed, along with the vine Prosecco, which represents the source material for the legendary, fashionable sparkling wines. The best Italian sparkling wine products come from the cultivated areas of Piemont, Lombardy, Venice and South Tyrol. A large share of Italian sparkling wines is produced by the vat fermentation production procedure. Having undergone the traditional bottle fermentation procedure, Spumante goes as "metodo classico" to the market. Light and succulent, Spumante is intended for quick consumption.

CAVA

The specification Cava was first established by the Spaniards in 1970, and it has its origin in Catalonia. Even today, about 90% of all Cavas are created here, mostly in San Sadurni de Noya and the surroundings areas. The typical Cava wine is a blend of relatively neutral Macabeo and fertile local Xarello grapes. In particular, its earthy aroma forms an essential feature of the classic Cava wine. It must be kept at least nine moths in yeast, under pressure of at least four atmospheres and with an alcohol content between 10.8 and 12.8%. The yields are set according to the following formula: 100 quarts per 331 lbs. The Spanish variants of the sparkling wine are produced, in most cases, according to the classic champagne method, for it can then be classified for the DO.

CLASSIFICATION

Extra Brut / Very Dry:
0 to 0.21 oz sugar per quart

Brut / Dry:
Below 0.52 oz sugar per quart

Extra dry / Extra Dry:
0.42 to 0.76 oz sugar per quart

Trocken / Dry / Secco / Asciutto:
0.6 to 1.23 oz sugar per quart

Half dry / Demi-Sec / Abboccato:
1.16 to 1.76 oz sugar per quart

Mild / Doux / Dolce:
1.76 oz sugar per quart and more.

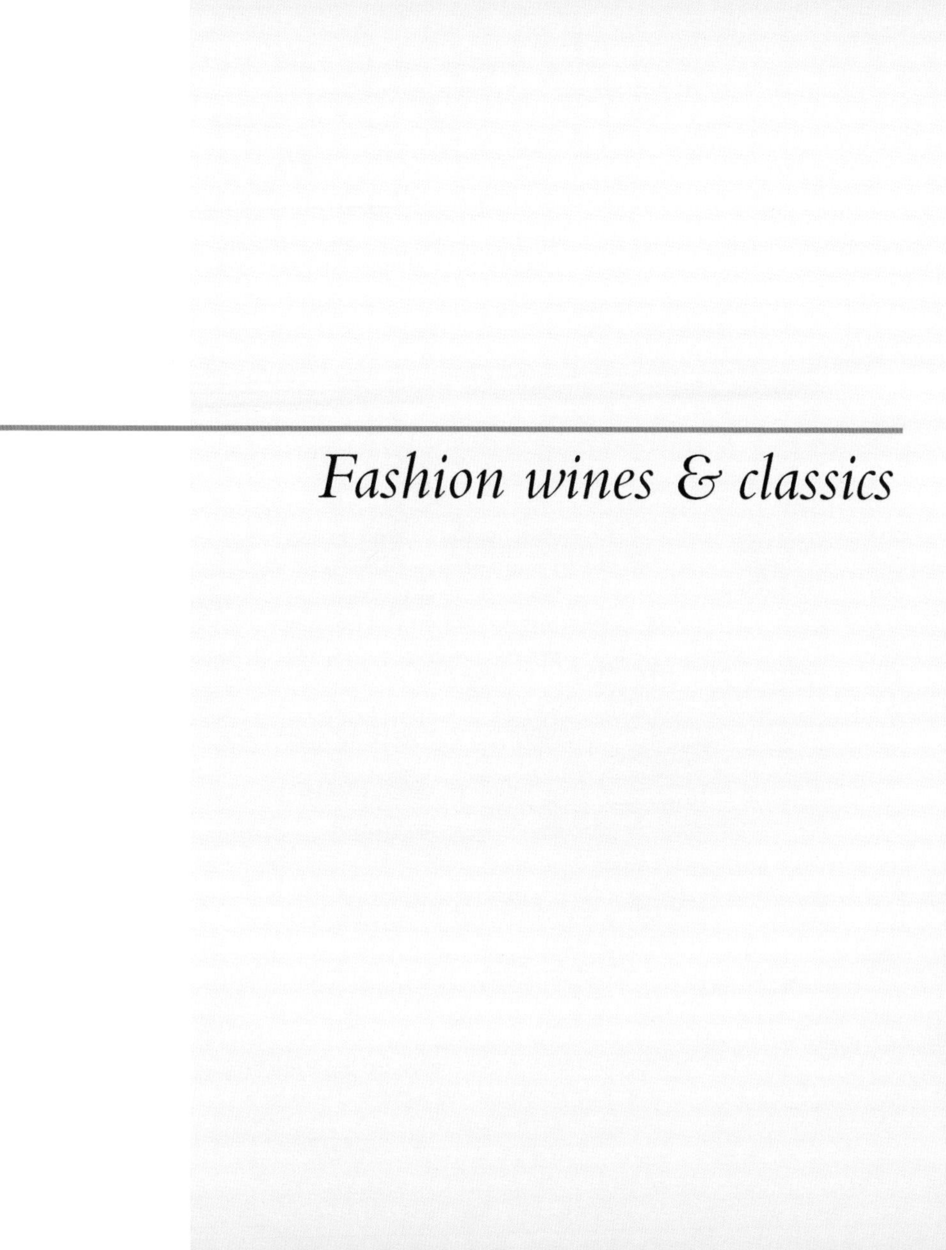

Fashion wines & classics

Fashion wines & classics

Nothing is more constant than change, although in a matter of drinking it is slower than in other fields. In the course of the centuries, the classics have been established and cannot be changed by their market position, frequently changing euphoria or by global fashion. What is apparent is that these culinary classics, with their cult character, come almost exclusively from France: Champagne, Bordeaux and Burgundy wines. It was only after the Second World War that other countries started to set trends which considerably influenced global drinking customs.

In matters of wine, the Germans were oriented towards domestic products for a long time. Only taste trends in wines were subject to change. Dry, fermented wines were replaced by sweet wines in the 1970s, and only regained their lost position in the middle of the 1980s. Followed by the disappearance of good home cooking, a foothold of German wine sales, and the introduction of new German top gastronomy, more foreign wines came into the market. The wine boom in America brought new types of wine, vines and growing methods to Germany. The Germans' love for travel is reflected in the vast variety of wines on the shelves of German supermarkets. No other country imports so extensive a variety of wines from around the world as Germany.

WINES MAKE CAREER

Some wines are starting to emerge as more than mere beverages or luxury items. The best examples are Bordeaux wines, which owe their comet-like rise to the English. The English were the first nation to import Bordeaux wines in a great style and enhanced the reputation of Bordelais as a winegrowing area.

This was also the case with Port and Sherry. Champagne, the epitome of sparkling luxury, had its first fans on the British Isle. The British and French are still regarded as the biggest champagne drinkers.

Rheingauer Riesling wines experienced a short boom in the middle of the 19th century. For these wines, kings and princes paid three times more than for Château Latour or Margaux. The First World War put an abrupt end to the success of the German wines. But Riesling wines are gradually becoming fashionable again since they are more wholesome and have a low alcohol content and are, therefore, ideal for light cuisine.

Italian wines, in particular Brunello di Montalcino and Chianti, have the same cult status as legendary Barbaresco and Barolo wines from Piemont, which is naturally reflected in the price.

Since the mid-1980s, American wines have climbed the career ladder. The Italian-American winegrower pioneer Robert Mondavi created "Opus One" with his Cabernet Sauvignon – in a joint production with the estate Rotschild and a rare cult wine from the Napa Valley.

Chardonnay from Burgundy, on the other hand, has considerably lost its image as a high quality white wine in recent years. All over the world, this type of vine has been sucessfully grown. America, particularly focused on mass instead of class, allowed Chardonnay – with strong wood aromas from the Barrique cask – to enter the market at bargain prices.

APERITIF AND DESSERT WINES

As no other drink, wine has a variety of flavors. Whereas simple wine belongs to everyday fare in most winegrowing regions, top wines only get into the glasses of a certain stratum of society. Apart from the versatile basic product, there are also unique specialties, gained either directly from the wine or from its fruit. Some of them are richer in alcohol than normal wines; others are extremely sweet and some can be stored for almost limitless periods. Aperitif and dessert wines are timeless classics in the wine world.

DESSERT WINE

When referring to large, noble, sweet wines, it is impossible not to encounter Sauternes. This dessert wine is a classic and has an intense, concentrated aroma and a stable sharpness which stand out in the world of noble sweet wines. Additionally, Sauternes wines can be 60 years old or even older, without losing their concentrated succulence. They are dependent on the noble rot that arises by means of the mushroom Botrytis cinerea. During the evaporation of water in the grapes, juice and sugar are concentrated. The longer the grapes hang, the more the grape shrinks, until it becomes a raisin. Consequently, a complex aroma arises, which is processed into noble wines in the region of Sauternes in Graves (Bourdeaux). Sauternes is a very demanding wine, since the grapes must be worked manually and carefully selected. Correspondingly, the yield is low, which is reflected in the price. The most famous Sauternes wine comes from the wine-growing estate Château d'Yquem and it is the only Sauternes classified among the first wines in the year 1855.

A bit to the south, on the steeply descending slopes of Roussillon in the direction of the Mediterranean Sea, a sweet wine grows which differs noticeably from the wines from Sauternes. In Banyuls-sur-Mer, Cerbère, Collioure and Port-Vendres, the renowned, spiked Vin Doux is produced. The wines –

The region of Sauternes covers five municipalities in the most southern part of Graves. The three permitted types of vine are Sémillion, Sauvignon Blanc and Muscadelle.

a blend of Grenache, Syrah and Carignan – are similar to port wine in their red-brown color and intense smell and are already spiked in the grape must. The Grand-Cru version must consist of at least 75% Grenache grapes and it is stored 30 months in a wooden cask.

Germany and Austria have known noble sweet wines for centuries and their intense aromas are greatly appreciated in those countries. Riesling, has abundant finesse, sharpness and varied grades of sweetness due to its components, namely dry wines made from specially selected grapes and sweet wines. The marvelous sweetness is accompanied by a unique finesse and variety of aromas, which, combined with the distinct sharpness of Riesling, balance and harmonize perfectly. Riesling sweet wines are also very durable.

EISWEIN – SWEET WINE

This sweet wine is regarded as a specialty which cannot be produced every year. The grapes hang longer on the vine and are exposed to the merciless weathering of the approaching winter. The game between the winegrower and nature can last through January and sometimes February. The courage of taking a risk is worth it: the wine, which is born during the coldest part of the winter, is wonderful.

Until 1982, the term Eiswein (sweet wine) did not match any quality. The corresponding quality specifications of late vintage and dry wines were added to the Eiswein specification. Following the amendment of the Wine Act, the Eiswein category was raised to a quality grade and the minimal must weight corresponding to the grape selection was specified.

Compared to other noble sweet wines and wines made from specially selected grapes, the secret of a noble wine lies in the dense concentration of grape substances and a relatively high level of acid. This phenomenon is achieved by freezing the grapes. At least 19°F is necessary, before the grapes can be selected as Eiswein, ideally it is from 14°F to 10°F. The naturally frozen grapes are pressed immediately.

As a result, water is bound and only the highly concentrated grape juice runs into the vats. It is then impossible to press more from the grapes. This gives quality before quantity. Passionate winegrowers of Eiswein pay careful attention to healthy vintage. For the required quality, the grapes should not be infested by the mold, Botrytis cinerea.

Cutting the vines and selection of grapes to reduce the yield volume is among the minimal requirements. Only about 10% of the original output quantity ends up in the bottle in the long run. The rest of the grape quantity is selectively excluded or becomes a victim of the unpredictable weather conditions.

PORT

It owes its name to the second largest city of Porto, Portugal, from which it has been shipped for more than 300 years by English business firms. Port is a sweeter, more alcoholic, brandy-spiked, fermented grape-must wine. There are two main categories of port: cask-aged or bottle-aged port wines from red or white grapes. The cask aged port wine is aged in wood and following clarification, filtration and filling is usually ready to drink. With regard to maturing in the bottle, port is refined for a short time in the cask and then filled into bottles without filtration. It can take as long as 30 years for the port to be fit for consumption.

There are more than 80 different types of wine permitted for use in port wine production. Most port is produced from the red wines: Touriga Nacional, Tinta Barroca, Touriga Francesa, Tinta Cão and Tinta Roriz (in Spain Tempranillo). Gouveio, Malvasia Fina and Viosinho are generally regarded as the best white grape types for port wine. Ruby Port is one of the simplest and cheapest styles of port, which is filled after only two or three years of aging. Tawny port is described as a port wine, which matures longer in the cask than Ruby and has an amber hue. Vintage port, the priciest port wine, is derived from the best, fully mature grapes, and hardly shows 1% age of the total turnover. As to Vintage, wines of a single vintage are blended and filled after two or three years of aging in the cask. At this time, the port begins to mature in thick and dark bottles. After 15 to 30 years, this port is fit for consumption, but it should be carefully served, since grounds have developed in the course of the years. Port wines are usually drunk as aperitifs; older vintages are suitable for sweet desserts.

SHERRY

The name Sherry – the anglicized form of the name Jerez – stands for an alcohol-enriched wine from Jerez de la Frontera in Andalusia. Within the region, there are three centers of Sherry preparation: Jerez de la Frontera, Sanlúcar de Barrameda and Puerto de Santa Maria. Sherry has two fundamental taste types: light, dry Fino and dark, dry Oloroso. All other Sherry styles, noted on the labels, refer to both these categories. In Jerez, only three types of vine are permitted for production: Palomino (95 % of the vine area), Pedro Ximénez and Muscat of Alexandria. Since the aphid infestation of the vine, all vines have been grafted onto the resistant American subsoil.

Depending on the style, Sherry is spiked with 15.5 to 22 percent alcohol. The creation of the yeast's strands, which differentiates Fino from other Sherry-styles, depends on the degree of the spike. With alcohol content of more than 16%, the growth of yeast is slowed down. Wines which should develop as Fino, are therefore maximally spiked to 15.5%.

Sherry Oloroso can take up to 18% of alcohol. Simpler Sherry-brands are a bit sweetened.

The yeast's strands, which protects the wine against oxidation and simultaneously preserves its character, must not die and is kept alive by means of the so-called Solera system for six years and longer. Sherry-Solera consists of several types of casks, which are only five sixths full. The Solera-principle creates a gradual blend of Sherry styles. It is generally filled from the cask that contains the oldest

SMALL STUDY OF TERMS

SCHNAPS: **a bit demeaning term for high percentage spirits, also known as distillers, which is not used in literature and orders.**

HARD DRINKS: **a generic term for drinks mostly composed of ethyl alcohol and water.**

DISTILLED LIQUORS: **hard drinks gained by means of distillation – or extraction of alcohol.**

BRAND: **hard drink gained by distilling the fermented must from fruits, grains, or roots.**

GEIST: **hard drink distilled from alcohol with aromatic berries, roots and herbs.**

LIQUOR: **hard drink, which is produced through aromatizing alcohol. All hard drinks which have a sugar content of more than 3½ oz per quart and an alcohol content of at least 15 volume percents, are called liquors.**

wine. The tapped quantity is then refilled from the casks of the previous level and so on. Sherry is mostly served as an aperitif.

GRAPPA – TRESTER – MARC

The spirit known as Tresterbrand in Germany, Marc in France, and Grappa in Italy is gained by the direct distillation of the skins of the pressed grapes.

The distillers differentiate between three main types: the pure natural, the half-fermented and the fermented marc. The pure, natural, non-fermented marc is a product of white wine production and it must ferment prior to distilling. Half of the fermented marcs usually come from the production of Rosato, the Italian rosé.

In most cases, fermented marcs processed for Grappa distillation, come from red wine grapes whose must is left until the complete termination of the fermentation. These marcs, due to long must contact, are refined by aromatic yeast and can be immediately distilled.

The Italian Grappa centers are situated in Friaul, Venetien and Piemont. The quality of the skins, the type of vine and the microclimate in the vineyard influence not only the wine, but also the Grappas, which result from the various variants.

Among the most interesting are individual Grappas produced from a single type of vine.

COGNAC

For a long time, Cognac was regarded as a symbol of French social and culinary culture. Recently, this classic has become less fashionable. Cognac comes from the distillation

The name Grappa is recognized by the EU, is legally protected and is used for distilled marc. The minimum alcohol content amounts to 37.5 volume percents.

of pure natural white wines, picked from the delimited French region Cognac with Départements Charente and Charente-Maritime. It owes its name to the name of the capital of the region. Cognac can be distilled according to the Charentaiser method, which includes the double distillation process – raw and fine distillation. Following the first distillation, the liquors are stored in oaken casks and the degree quality is determined. It can only be be distilled from the beginning of the wine vintage until 31 March of the following year. In the course of storing, 4% of the alcohol evaporates annually from the casks (about 23 million bottles, double the quantity exported to Germany). This evaporation is also called "la part des anges" – the angel's share.

All distilled wines produced in the course of the distillation period begin their first year of cask storing on 1 April. The age of the Cognac depends exclusively on the mature vintage in the cask. Cognac does not develop any longer in the bottle. The age of Cognac is controlled by the BNIC (Bureau National Interprofessionnel du Cognac) only at the end of the sixth year.

BRANDY OR COGNAC?

Brandy belongs to the oldest alcoholic distilled liquors in Europe. Its can be traced back to the 12th century, when the first wine distillation was documented. Until the end of the First World War, brandy was called Cognac in German-speaking countries. For the first time, in the Treaty of Versailles, this specification was banned and reserved only for French products from similarly named winegrowing regions. Since then, the term "brandy" has once again gained market significance. In France, brandies are usually called "Fine," provided they do not come from Cognac or Armagnac.

SMALL SCIENCE OF COGNAC

- Fine champagne: a blend of Grande Champagne-distillates with brands from Petite Champagne.
- VS (Very Superior) ***: When the youngest distillate is up to 4½ years, Cognac as VS or *** may be graded.
- VSOP (Very Superior Old Pale): The age of the youngest distillate is between 4½ and 6½ years.
- XO, Napoléon, Extra, Hors d'Age: it is the youngest distillate over 6½years old, and can carry the specification of Cognac.

Everything practical

DOMECQ
DOMECQ
DOMECQ
Alexander Fleming
June 10 '48
DOMECQ
G. Marañon
5-1-55
DOMECQ
DOMECQ
F. Jardiel Poncela
Febrero 1944
Wellington
y
Ciudad Rodrigo
1995

Everything practical

Buying – but where?

The constantly increasing variety of wine evokes the question: where can you buy the best wine? Wine is not only on everyone's lips today, but it can also be found in excess in food branches – at gas stations, in simple groceries around the corner, in department stores or in city wine shops with a tasting department.

In winegrowing estates, delicatessens and wine shops, you can get the best advice. Former sommeliers who are familiar with wine, if not experts, often work there. Wines are properly tempered and classified to qualities. There-

fore it is best to buy wine with a wine expert on hand, so that you avoid unpleasant surprises and taste confusions.

The person who buys his wine exclusively at supermarkets can simply reach for a wine from the wine shelf, but what is missing here is professional consultation. It is best to find your bearings according to the vintage, the type of vine or the country of the producer. Try all regions until you find the right taste. About 20,000 winegrowing estates and winegrowers' organizations in the German speaking areas fill the bottles, but most sell their products directly to the individual customer.

Compare the prices. You often cannot find an expensive bottle with an equally good content. Do not be dazzled by the appearance – good wines can often be found in inconspicuous bottles with inconspicuous labels. To find your way around the domestic and international wine world, read relevant wine guides. With their advice, you can plan a weekend trip to a wine region.

Buying a wine is largely a matter of trust, but certain aspects should be taken into account, especially when you search for high quality wines. Whether in the supermarket or the specialized shop, wines are sensitive and finding a good one requires a meticulous, time-consuming search.

An optimal storeroom should have a temperature of about 54°F and humidity of at least 60%. Some wine cellars show even 100% humidity and that brings about mold. A humid climate is good for wine because the humidity keeps the corks fresh and elastic. In dry rooms, or in rooms in commercial establishments, overheated due to lamps

and spotlights, the cork can quickly become dry, leaky and crumbly. The wine evaporates faster and the wine oxidizes and becomes undrinkable. Wines filled to just below the neck of the bottle can be problematic and should be carefully consumed.

Be careful with dusty bottles. Such wines are best bought only where a lot is known about old wines. Some sellers specialize in rarities and know the history and origin of the wine and can also provide expertise. An unusually low price for an old wine is also suspicious. True treasures are not cheap and have their own price depending on the existent availability and age. Do not go for bargains when buying old wines.

Keep away from bottles which have been on the shelves for many years. Only fresh and young wines are stored standing, they enter the market directly following filling and are intended for quick consumption. In any case, older vintages should be stored on their side.

MEETING DEMANDS

More than ever, wines are offered now that are meant for fast and immediate consumption. Most wines are meant to go from the supermarket shelf to the fridge and then straight to the table without problems. You do not have to equip your house or apartment with wine vaults. Simple everyday wines, characterized by tasty freshness, can endure days and weeks in the fridge or in relatively warm cellars without any problems.

Good everyday wines – usually priced between $6 to $9 – can last up to one year. At that point, they should be consumed because they will not get better. With higher price classes and quality grades, the opposite holds true: the better the wine, the longer it takes to reach full maturity and the more valuable it will be when fully mature. It should be stored professionally.

Since wine is a living product, it responds naturally to physical setting. For storage of one year, aired cellars with

a humidity of 70 to 90% are the most suitable. The cellar should have a more or less constant temperature between 50 and 60°F all year round. The warmer the cellar, the quicker the wine loses its freshness. Its maturity and ageing process is carried out faster in a colder storeroom.

Wine should always be stored in the dark because light can instigate unpleasant, premature aging. It is also important to remember that bottles should be stored on their side to moisten the cork.

Thus the bottleneck remains closed and the air penetration, which could lead to harmful oxidation, is avoided. For storing in an apartment or in a small cellar room, there are wine-air-climate shelves, similar to a fridge, which facilitate maintaining a constant temperature for top quality wines. Such gadgets are available in specialized stores.

WELL-TEMPERED

In magnum bottles, the wine ages a bit slower; in smaller bottles, the wine matures faster and loses its substance quicker.

Whether a wine tastes right or not depends decisively on the correct temperature. If wines are too cold, they cannot develop their aromas properly; they are reserved and more or less tasteless to the palate. Very volatile bouquet substances are still perceptible, yet flavor and extracts can hardly be perceived. On the other hand, wines presented too warm are mostly overloaded, heavy and tend to lack elegance.

Moderate wine tempering should take place. A quick, high cooling is not recommended, nor is a sudden warming of the wine. The ideal temperature is usually difficult to define: a well-considered average plays a decisive role with the correct tempering. Naturally, there is a certain range to which you should conform. The time of year when the wine is drunk plays a role. On a hot summer day, a white wine tastes best a couple of degrees colder. Rosé wine is nice when icy cold.

For sparkling wines, a temperature of 46° and 50°F is recommended. White wines of simple and medium quality are optimally tempered between 50° and 52°F. A high quality wine should is best between 54° and 55°. With red wine tempering, room temperature is best. Originally, "room temperature" meant the temperature of the room heated by the fireplace, i.e. with the temperature between 59° and 64°F. Young, light wines taste colder when served at temperatures between 50° and 55°F.

If you want to be certain, use a wine thermometer to find the right temperature. You should also consider the fact that wine placed close to warm meals can warm up relatively quickly. A sect bucket, filled with ice, or a wine cooler will keep it the right temperature.

THE RIGHT OVERVIEW

Wine should principally be drunk from one glass. For all various glass forms and types several basic rules are valid: colored glasses belong in the glass cabinet and they are not appropriate for wine degustations. A wineglass should be clear so that the color of the wine is easily perceived. Crystal cut itself can affect the assessment of the color brilliance. The color of the glass has no influence on its taste.

On the other hand, the glass form determines how the wine meets the tongue and its taste zones. The bigger the goblet and the thinner the glass, the more easily aromas and taste are perceived. The less wine in the glass, the more intense the aroma after the glass is slightly shaken.

Light white wines are best drunk from narrow glasses. Through the tapered off goblet, tender smells are compressed and driven to the nose, the tongue and the palate. Full-bodied white wines and older wines require, on the other hand, some space in the glass and larger, more bulbous glasses are better.

Quality sweet wines are nice in smaller glasses, due to their extreme thickness and high concentration of aromatic substances. Through the relatively thin opening, the wine is driven directly over the top of the tongue to emphasize the sweetness.

For red wines, medium-sized glasses, which get thinner towards the top, should be used. Heavy, older red wines are best drunk from a glass with a large diameter so that the wine surface comes into contact with the air. Richness and complexity can thus develop optimally. The relatively wide opening of the glass drives the wine to all taste nerves in the mouth and ideally frames succulence and sharpness. The high chimney drives aromas in a concentrated manner to the nose and the wine is tasted first on the top of the tongue.

UNCORKING AND DECANTING

Many promising wines have been ruined during uncorking. The trickiness of uncorking lies in the details. There are several methods for successfully removing the firmly stuck cork from the neck of the bottle: pulling, levering, twisting, air pressure or the automatic bottle screw. The safest and easiest method is the good, old corkscrew. You should make sure that the corkscrew is not similar to a drill, but rather has an open spiral whose inner convolutions are large enough to put a match through. The corkscrew should have a sharp point which follows the course of the spiral and is not centered.

The corkscrew should be cleanly driven into the cork and you should grab it firmly so that it does not crumble when it is pulled out. Should the cork crumbs get into the wine bottle, pour the wine through a fine sieve into the decanter. When the wine – particularly older wines – show dregs or deposits that have developed in the course of time on the bottom of the bottle, sieving is especially recommended. If the wine stone in the bottle is visible, the wine should also be decanted, so that the drinking pleasure is not spoiled

Whether or not wines would be better if not decanted, due to drafts, is still controversial among experts. The effects of sudden contact between oxygen and the wines depend primarily on the age and the quality of the wine. Young, tannin-rich red wines are decanted so that the wine can breathe and get rid of unpleasant tangs. More

mature wines – red or white – lose all their aromas after staying in the decanter – and that is considerably more than in a concentrated manner from the bottle. How long and which wine should stay opened, is still not expressly defined.

The most reasonable method is to taste the wine several times following the decanting so that the developing stages of the wine in the air are observed.

An opened bottle should be used within three days. Unfinished bottles of wine – especially Champagne and sects – should simply not lie around because aromas evaporate in the course of time and foreign smells can spoil the wine. In cases where the original cork cannot close the bottle, there are a series of other closing alternatives, but they are temporary solutions and are not intended to accommodate longer storage.

THERE'S NOTHING LIKE TASTING

No other foodstuff offers such a taste variety as wine. Wines come from all over the world and a new vintage appears every year. Correspondingly, a variety of wines can be procured from a specialist, or in food and liquor stores or directly from the producer. A good wine is a matter of taste and occasion, mood and, naturally, sensibility.

Personal preference is established by tasting. Whether you have a full wine cellar or the wine goes directly from the shopping bag to the table, the choice of the wine is entirely up to you. Those unfamiliar with wine should allow themselves to be advised in wine shops. Each larger department store has a competent wine department with wines from all over the world. But be careful: the bargain chase is for advanced connoisseurs! Wine is a foodstuff and you should taste it, not look at the price.

Those who want to taste wines should taste according to various criteria: e.g. the area of origin, independent of the vintage and the type of vine. Or you should select the same type of vine from various growing areas, e.g. Chardonnay, and then take a trip through Europe and America. Tasting wines according to their vintages can be quite expensive. Some vintages are already sold out and you will have to dig deep into your pocket for rarities. The following applies to wine tasting: start with the youngest vintages and continue in descending order. Red wines and white wines should not be drunk at the same time.

For degustation, the glass is filled to one third with wine, for a meal, two thirds are enough.

WHAT EXACTLY MAKES A SOMMELIER?

The more wines on the menu in a European restaurant, the greater the resulting confusion. A sommelier usually provides competent advice because he is a specialist in harmonizing wine and food. A sommelier is accountable for the care of the wine cellar and he must know the particular winegrowing regions, buy wines, observe their mature state and recommend wines for individual courses to the chief chef. The sommelier is someone as talented in culinary pleasures as the chef.

Misuse of the term 'sommelier' has lead to uncertainties and devaluation of the job image.

In order to understand clearly and distinctly the job specification and to make the requirements of the sommelier uniformly and transparent for the public, the German Sommelier Union (Deutsche Sommelier Union) has introduced the protected job title "Sommelier SU." Prerequisites for becoming a sommelier are: a creditable education, minimal requirements of work experience and passing a demanding exam, which entitles you to be "Sommelier SUA." Knowledgeable and professional sommeliers can be indispensable advisers in a confusing, constantly changing world of wines.

Harmony between wine & food

Château
Vieux Rocs

Harmony between wine & food

Pleasure in its truest sense is on everyone's lips for good reason. In the past few years, cellars and kitchens have been revolutionized by young winegrowers and despite all the rules, whatever you enjoy is permitted. This is the credo of a new lifestyle and its success is manifested in new wine varieties.

The variety of domestic and international wines has never ever been as extensive as it is today. It offers an enormous selection to the consumer as well as unknown and completely new combination possibilities. Tasting the world through its wines, harmonizing wines and food and placing delight in the foreground, are the criteria that determine wine selection today. Quality is taken for granted. It is no longer a matter of trends. "Drinking experience" is celebrated. When dealing with wines as food, lifestyle and culture come to the forefront. Good taste cannot be prescribed and each of us must discover our own favorites and preferences. Try simple new things, be courageous and experiment with food and drinks. In the end, you will find wine and foods that complement each other. Even if you have little experience, you can enrich your delight spectrum and identify your delight threshold with the first bite and sip.

WHICH WINE WITH WHICH MEAL?

Get ready to experiment. The days when white wine was exclusively served with white meat and venison was only accompanied by red wine are gone forever. Following the breakthrough of new, creative cuisine and the growing success of Asian food, we appeal to well-assorted cellars. Varied wines match aromatic meals, fantasy combinations of delight and taste in star restaurants. Tastes might be different, but there are certain, irrefutable rules when finding an ideal combination of wine and food: food and drinks should be similar in their primary flavors. Only when ingredients and preparations complement the smell and aroma substances of the wine, is an appropriate wine found. Food and drinks should complement each other so that one does not dominate or cover up the taste of the other one. The secret of sensual, culinary delight lies in the harmonious, aromatic rapport between the wine and the meal.

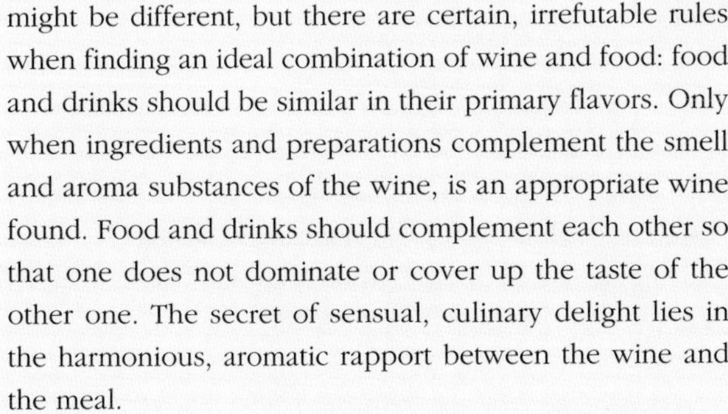

Riesling wines usually have an acidic content distinctly higher than in other types of vine. The perception of acid irritates especially the tip of the tongue, but also the inner mucous membranes of the cheeks. It instigates a plentiful flow of saliva since acids multiply in taste perception. Riesling wines, rich in acid, therefore do not match sharp meals such as Rhine roast sirloin or meals with a distinct lemon taste. As for acid, it does not depend much on quantity, but rather on the ration of acidity to sweetness: sugar and acid must be harmoniously balanced. It is recommended to drink a milder wine, a late vintage with residual sugar, with acidic meals. Wine acid also intensifies bitter substances and natural spices. The sweeter the wine, the more it can balance bitter flavors and spicy touches, providing the palate with a harmonious taste. If possible, the wine should possess a high alcohol content which emphasizes the sweet taste.

Festive food – festive wines

Geese, ducks and turkeys belong to the most favorite festive roast dishes – classically served with red cabbage, chestnuts, marzipan, apple and potato dumplings. It is not easy for a wine, in particular a white wine, to find a common ground with this opulent and substantial flavor collection.

Someone who wants to drink white wine with poultry should select a substantial and full-bodied wine. Gewürztraminer or Tokay Pinot Gris from Alsace, Chablis or mature Chardonany from overseas, is wonderful with fat roast geese. But normally, a full-bodied, sharp red wine is recommended: Spätburgunder from Baden or St. Laurent from Burgundy. Those who want to give festive goose a touch of savoir vivre should have Burgundy wines from Vosne-Romanée, Vougeot or Pommard. Naturally, wines from Bordelais cut a good figure for a goose, as well as the Italian classics such as Barolo, Barbaresco, Chianti Classico Riserva and Vino da Tavola from Toscana. Pinotage from South Africa, Merlot from Chile or California and Cabernet Sauvignon from Australia, are ranked among the established goose companions.

Turkey, filled with sharp ground meat or fruits, represents a low fat alternative to the roast goose and the duck is becoming, little by little, a holiday meal. Red roasted duck breast with crispy skin is still the most popular duck dish.

Carp, the other hand, has never actually become a festive food in Germany. Fish seems rather an exception on a holiday menu. It is astonishing because this healthy food from rivers and seas offers plenty of possibilities for people who love to cook.

In the culinary harmony between fish and wine, there are ideal combinations including light Riesling wines from Rheingau or elegant Grau and Weißburgunder from the Bad vineyards near Kaiserstuhl. Young, sweet quality wines from Mosel, Saar and Ruwer make the fish even tastier and will simultaneously make your mouth water.

For those who seek to break away from familiar holiday traditions, a series of interesting gourmet delights, showing the holidays in a new culinary light, is emerging.

"European-Asian trend" is a magic phrase. More and more European top cooks support this trend and offer a combination of traditional European cuisine prepared with Asian preparation methods and Asian spice varieties in their restaurants. Asian spices, such as roasted Sichuan-peppercorns, madras-curry powder, sternanis, cloves, ginger and cinnamon give grilled pork chop a totally new taste and offer guests a pleasant change from domestic cuisine. Moreover, when the cook knows how to use a wok, the variants of the side dishes are unlimited.

European winegrowers support this European-Asian gourmet boom as well and have seen a renaissance in their top quality sweet wines. German white wines with perceptible residual sugar, particularly late vintages, perfectly connect with the European-Asian palate, creating magic with a tasty symbiosis between sweetness and sharpness.

We must also mention sushi. Japanese cuisine has a lot to offer. However, it takes a long time for a cook to prepare the meals. Top quality Riesling wines from Mosel and from Rheingau, but also the succulent Sheugrape from Pfalz, Rieslaner from the Würzburger Weinbergen or Riesling selections from Roter Hang near Nackenheim complete the festive meals in a culinary manner.

Whether you opt for classic geese, turkeys, ducks or for European-Asian wok-prepared meals, every meal becomes festive if it is eaten accompanied by the appropriate wines.

DESSERTS AND CHRISTMAS SWEETS WITH WINE

Christmas baking encompasses a whole series of aromas: cinnamon, raisin, marzipan, almonds and ginger are the most taste intensive ingredients of gingerbread, gingerbread biscuits, finely bitter small chocolate biscuits with layers of marzipan and gingerbread, marzipan bread, biscuit, vanilla croissant, pie, macaroons and cinnamon flavored star-shaped biscuits. What does one drink then with these culinary temptations? Symbiosis between wine and desserts and sweets is not evident at first glance, but requires instinctive feeling. The aromas of the wine should harmonize with the ingredients of desserts. No easy task for the wine.

For a long time, people believed that no wine could appropriately match chocolate, until Banylus from French Languedoc proved the contrary. Since then, other strong alcoholic wines have been paired with chocolate desserts. While tasting various types of wine with desserts and Christmas baking, think of Amaretto, which came out first in Vino Santo and tastes great and still constitutes an exciting, aromatic experience. And finally, numerous German dessert wines are divine desserts in themselves. However, be careful with bitter chocolate. Sweet wines already contain some bitter substances due to Botrytis, which adds bitter aromas to choco-

late and can dominate the taste. The wine should contain a high alcohol and sweet content, so that the bitter substances of the chocolate are covered up.

It is not a problem in the case of full cream milk chocolate, for the bitter substances are reduced by means of purification. As for other deserts, there is rule of thumb which should be understood merely as a recommendation. With Christmas cookies which contain sternanis, cinnamon or clove and have strong aromas, match relatively full-bodied wines such as Gewürztraminer or Muskateller. The wine should bring out some sweetness. Sweet late vintages or sweet quality wines such as Sélection de Grains Nobles from Alsace are best combined with classic Christmas baking. If fruits are used with a dessert or confectionery, the accompanying sweet wine should have a proper sharpness. Here, Riesling vintages or wines made from specially selected grapes from Germany or Alsace are recommended. Heavy desserts prepared with a great deal of butter should be combined with heavy wines. Strong Ruländer vintages or sweet wines made from specially selected grapes, Sauternes wines or Tokay Pinot Gris Sélection de Grains Nobles balance the heavy desserts. Rich and concentrated dry wines made from specially selected grapes and Eiswines from German vineyards are always worth tasting and are suitable with homemade Christmas cakes as well as gingerbread.

WINE & MINERAL WATER BY MARKUS DEL MONEGO, WORLD SOMMELIER EXPERT

Wine and water are often paired. Obviously, you can mix these drinks as a spritzer. However, a glass of mineral water next to the wine glass is a must. First, our body needs water in order to regulate itself and alcohol is dehydrating. Mineral water washes the palate and taste buds, neutralizes them and prepares the senses for a new taste experience.

The actual taste of mineral water is not often perceptible the first time, but it is noticeably discerned in harmony with a characteristic wine. Mineral water can bring out interesting features in the wine or it can deprive it of its taste. Not every mineral water tastes similarly with each wine. The mineral matter mixture and the sweet-acid-aroma combination must complement each other.

One rule of thumb declares that wine and mineral water can go together, provided that they are from the same region and come from the same soil, which determines their mineral composition and tastes. But be careful: mineral water and wine should be relished separately. Generally referring to the content of carbon acid, we can claim that mineral water with less carbon acid subordinates itself easily to the wine and the menu. However, less carbon acid in the mineral water is not homologous with the taste of the wine. The harmony of mineral water and wine becomes more complex at this point. The motto remains: taste to increase your knowledge.

The following rules are only clues to successful individual mineral water and wine combination:

- Strongly mineralized water can accentuate tannin substances and acids in the wine while simultaneously reducing the wine's sweetness and luster.
- Strong acid water with a lot of carbon acids will slightly strengthen tannin substances and mitigate the sweetness of the wine. Acids, depending on the content of the wine, come out feebly or more intensively.
- Strong alkaline water (with high acid carbonate content) will mitigate tannin substances and acid. The danger: wine can lose its character quickly and become bland and one dimensional.
- The more neutral the water (i.e. if it contains few mineral matters, acids or bases), the less the various components in the wine change.

BORDEAUX WINE TIP BY MARKUS DEL MONEGO

Bordeaux, the largest cultivated area of quality wines in France, has a great quantity of wine styles to offer, which allow versatile and different application possibilities in gastronomy. The great red wines are the most famous representatives of a long French wine culture and are available in two completely different styles:

The wines from the left Gironde shore, from Graves or Médoc, for instance, are strongly marked by the Cabernet Sauvignon vine. These young, tannin-rich wines can be combined with braised meals or with substantial grilled Entrecôte (ideally grilled on the Cabernet Sauvignon grape – which gives it a special flavor). In addition, a classic Bordelaise sauce can be served, which brings out the tannin flavor of the young wines with its strong character. The more mature Cabernet Sauvignon wines suit fine cuisine perfectly. Fillet of beef, with a touch of truffles, but also roasted doves or quails harmonize perfectly. No one can resist cheese soufflé accompanied by red Bordeaux. The so-called "Boule de Lille" or "Mimolette" cheese specialties, which resemble Dutch Gouda, are best accompanied by a great wine from Médoc or Graves.

The wines from the right Giornde shore, from Saint-Emilion, Pomerol, Fronsac and the surrounding municipalities, owe their character to the vine Merlot. These wines are often a bit mellower and also more amenable than the wines from the left shore. Young wines from the Merlot grape often smell of small red fruits and red currant. Roast substances must be used here to calm the tannin character of the wine. The wines harmonize with a substantial tureen as well as with profuse ragout or with any other grilled classic Entrecôte. Mature wines, mainly from Pomerol and Saint-Emilion, harmonize absolutely with meals which contain exotic, mild spices. Venison also benefits from a Merlot based wine. The combination of a mature wine, containing little tannin and strong body, with a bitter chocolate dessert such as chocolate soufflé, is almost magical.

According to the producers of sweet wines from Bordeaux, their sweet treasures do not go well with food. However, these top wines harmonize perfectly with many desserts based on vanilla, caramel, apples, pears, apricots, cherries and exotic fruits, and also come out excellently with pâté de foie gras. They also eliminate the pungency of blue cheese and lose a bit of their ostentation and cuteness at the same time. A combination of monkfish baked in paprika or pheasant breast with pâté de foie gras sauce is definitely worth trying. Sweet wines from Bordeaux are not suited for sweet meals.

The dry white wines are divided in two categories. Wines from steel vessels charm with their intense and refreshing taste. They make sushi and sashimi a delight and can accompany veal or fish as well. At the same time, in combination with light fish dishes, they are forceful and also can ennoble fresh goat's milk cheese.

White wines aged in the Barrique have a more intense and fuller character, which is often tinged by roast aromas of the small French wood cask. Fish and shellfish are suitable here as well as roasted or grilled sea food.

Red or white, dry or sweet, succulently aged in the steel vessel or ennobled with the roast aromas in the Barrique: the range of wine styles in Bordeaux is immense, fascinating and can accompany almost each dish in the world.

BON APPETIT – ET BON SOIF! RED WINE FOR A MEAL: SPÄTBURGUNDER, BY JAN BIMBOES, FREELANCE COLLABORATOR FROM SOMMELIER CONSULT, AND SOMMELIER FOR THE WINE STORE NICOLAY & SCHARTNER, STUTTGART

The most versatile red vine type is Spätburgunder, depending on the terroir where this demanding vine grows. Provided one is familiar with the succulent, marmalade like Spätburgunder grown in sunny regions, Spätburgunder wines from colder areas are spicy, mineral and individual.

Characteristics of Spätburgunder wines include intensive aromas of juniper, blackberry, sour cherry and black pepper harmonized with fine tannin substances. After swallowing, it leaves a fine, bitter almond touch.

In order to harmonize your meal with wine, a little spice and herbs should be used. Products roasted crispy – notably lamb steak, wild boar ragout or beef steak – have their own particular taste and are not suited for Spätburgunder. Spätburgunder should be served with mild dishes such as venison ragout or duck breast. Because of its fine fruit aromas, mild spice and smooth body, Spätburgunder is an ideal companion for fish dishes. Red wine and fish with Spätburgunder is a special taste, but worth a try in any case.

WINE & BARBECUE BY GÖTZ DREWITZ VINOMATION, WINE ADVISOR

As soon as the grilling season starts, there is smoke curling into the air above every backyard. A cold beer is mostly drunk with tidbits from the grill and wine does not seem to match the rustic taste and aromas of a barbecue. But this is a mistake: lamb carrée, beef fillet steaks or steaks with rosemary, thyme and black pepper will find an appropriate culinary companion in the wine world. What about a strong, succulent, woody and tannin-sweet wine from overseas?

The smoky roast aromas of steak harmonize best with the pleasant Barrique aromas of Australian Shiraz or South-African Pinotage wines. Both wines contain a perceptible, but silky tannin touch, which complements gravy drizzled over a medium roasted fish. The more rosemary used during grilling, the spicier the aromas of Pinotage. In the case of side-dishes, both strong wines cut a good figure. Pinotage or different Australian Shiraz wines are delicious with rosemary Ratatouille and potatoes in olive oil, spiced with sea salt, nutmegs and a lot of rosemary.

Sashimi from tuna fish

KATJA GIESSLER MANAGER OF FISCHERS WEINGENUSS & TAFELFREUDEN RESTAURANT

INGREDIENTS: 8 slices of tuna fish (Lions Sushi-quality) • pepper • 1 tablespoon olive oil • 1 lb bamboo shoots • ¾ oz Julienne carrots • 4 teaspoons sugar peas • 1 tablespoon sesame oil • 1 Balsamic spritzer • 1 oz Ketjap Manis • salt • 1 coriander sprout • 1 teaspoon sesame, black and white • 3½ tablespoons Crème fraîche • 4 teaspoons melted cream • juice and skins from 1 lemon • 1 tablespoon lemon olive oil • 4 cherry tomatoes • sesame for garnishing

PREPARATION: Cut thin slices of tuna fish, spice it with pepper and sear it sharply on one side in oil. Turn slightly the bamboo shoots and the steamed Julienne from potatoes and sugar capsules in the pan with sesame oil and baste it with Balsamic vinegar. Then spice it with a bit of Ketjap manis, pepper and salt. Finally, mix it with coriander and sesame.

Stir the lemon sauce with Crème fraîche, cream, lemon olive oil, lemon juice and lemon cysts.

Stack the tuna fish slices with the raw sides upwards in the shoot salad. Drizzle the lemon juice around the meal. Finally, spread some sesame over the sauce and garnish it with steamed cherry tomatoes.

THE SUITABLE WINE: Asian dishes and sweet wines: the combination is not new. Young Riesling wines in particular, with their fine citrus and grapefruit aromas and light succulence, ideally match, according to my taste, the intense taste of Asian spices.

A young sweet Rheingauer Riesling with sashimi from tuna fish and with Asian shoot salad, lemon juice and black sesame: the sweetness of the wine binds the saltiness of soy sauce and produces an aroma of roasted fish and vegetables. Everything is harmonious in the mouth: tasty Riesling sharpness gives it something different and complements the taste buds. The meal is very refreshing due to the combination with Riesling.

Partridge in honey whiskey sauce

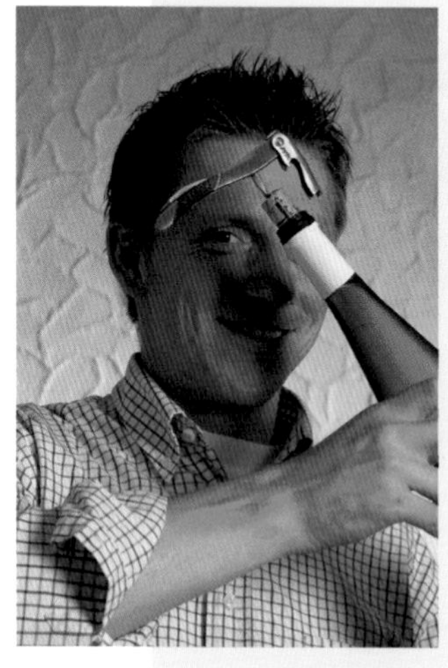

CHRISTIAN FRENS SOMMELIER FISCHERS WEINGENUSS & TAFELFREUDEN

INGREDIENTS: 1 partridge (about 3½ lbs) • 1 lb shallot in slices • 3 tablespoons coarse-grained mustard (Dijon-mustard) • 2 bay leaves • 2 oz shallot cubes • 1 tablespoon butter • 3 tablespoons gravy • 2 tablespoons honey • 4 tablespoons cream • 1 small thyme sprout • 1 small rosemary sprout • 3 tablespoons whiskey • 1 lb celery sprigs • 4 tablespoons butter • 7 tablespoons cream • 3 tablespoons coarse-grained mustard • salt and pepper

PREPARATION: Salt and pepper the partridge inside with shallot, add some spoons of mustard and bay leaf. Bake the whole about 45 minutes at 329°F in the oven.

Briefly fry shallot cubes in butter for the sauce and baste with gravy. Stir some spoons of honey with cream, add herbs and let it cook. Season with whiskey according to taste and remove herbs shortly before serving. Fry vegetables in some butter, pour in some cream and season with a bit of salt and pepper.

THE SUITABLE WINE: Creamy sauces require wines with a perceptible body and strong resonance. A high amount of sharpness in the wines would be certainly disturbing and would leave a bitter impression in the mouth if combined with naturally fat cream.

A wine from the vine Chenin Blanc has gained new respect and can be ranked among the most characteristic white wines of the world. The wines sparkle and have a lively, but full-bodied sharpness and structure and, with their exotic aromas of blossom, quince, honey and underbrush, keep a sparkling balance with the honey-based sauce. The creamy composition of Chenin Blanc emphasizes the flavor of poultry.

TIP

Never serve this wine cold, please! It will be just fine, if you decant this "muscle man" before starting the proper baking. The resulting wine will thank you in its phenomenal way.

Sweet sour duck

Astrid Müllers Business manager of Sommelier-Consult in Cologne

Ingredients: ½ lb breast duck filet • salt, pepper • 6 dry Chinese morels • 2 shallots • 1 red and 1 yellow paprika • 2 red chilli husks • ½ pineapple • 1 small mango • 4 tablespoons oil • 1 teaspoon grated fresh ginger • 1 tablespoon honey • 1 teaspoon curry • 2 tablespoons soy sauce • 1 tablespoon Aceto balsamico • 1 tablespoon Fino-Sherry • 1 teaspoon cornstarch

Preparation in the wok: Rinse and dry the breast of duck, cut into medium-sized cubes and season with salt and pepper. Dip in lukewarm water for four minutes. Peel shallots and cut into quarters, cleanse paprika, remove skins and strips. Clean chilies and cut into rings. Peel and cube pineapple and mango.

Warm up the oil in the wok and fry the cubes of duck breast briefly. Take them out, fry briefly shallots, paprika and chilies. After few minutes, add fruits and drained mushrooms. Mix ginger, honey and curry. Whip soy sauce, vinegar, and sherry and mix. Simmer everything and add the crunchy duck cubes. Warm it until the meat is finished and still rose-colored. Serve sweet sour Basmati rice with the duck.

THE SUITABLE WINE: it is not easy to find an appropriate wine for Asian cuisine. The concentrated exotic spices, fruits and sweetness should be considered when choosing the wine. Full-bodied wines such as robust-succulent Riesling wines are simply perfect. They have a piquant play on the tongue. A wine with sweetness, e.g. a late vintage from Mosel-Saar-Ruwer or a succulent Riesling sweet wine from Pfalz is also nice. And there is another type: muscatel. The harmonious sweetness of the wine is reminiscent of elegant fruits and even has aromas of pineapple and mango. A glimmer of muscatel can keep up with the roast duck and highlights the sweet and sour sauce.

SWEET-SOUR DUCK

Sweet-sour duck – two words that conjure up quickly a feeling of Asia at home, especially if you add a couple of exotic spices and healthy ingredients. Asian cuisine won a permanent position in people's hearts a long time ago. Especially dishes from the wok are popular and present an optical delight for the cook and guests.

Gâteau au Chocolat

CHRISTINE BALAIS SOMMELIER, FREELANCE COLLABORATOR FROM SOMMELIER CONSULT

INGREDIENTS: 4 oz salted butter • 4 oz slightly bitter chocolate • 6 oz sugar • 2 eggs • 5 tablespoons flour • 1 spread teaspoon baking powder • cracked walnuts at will • confectioner's sugar for sprinkling on top

PREPARATION: Melt butter and chocolate in the microwave oven or in the double boiler. Add sugar and stir everything well in the blender. Then, stir the eggs into the mass and finally add flour and baking powder. At the end, mix the cracked walnuts in the greased baking tin, coated with flour, with the prepared dough. Bake the cake at 356°F for about 25 minutes. Attention: Do not bake too long. The cake must remain soft and moist. Let it cool a bit before cutting and sprinkle with confectioner's sugar.

TIP
Do not bake this cake too long! It should remain soft and moist inside.

THE SUITABLE WINE: The cake is a typical finale in French cuisine. This fancy chocolate cake is marked by slightly bitter chocolate and nuts. Sweet wine is the appropriate counterpart. Wines made from specially selected grapes from the spicy vines Ruländer, Gewürztraminer or Muskat are ideally suited for chocolate cake and the fruity sweetness and aroma of the wine and cake melt together. Great combinations are also represented by sweet stored wines such as Port wine, Madeira or sweet Sherry.

However, my favorite wine for Gâteau au Chocolat is the wine from the southern French region Roussillon, pressed from the Grenache vine: Banyuls is dark, heavy wine with at least 15.5 % alcohol and is ideal for the chocolate cake, not least because of its complementary color. Its intense aromas are very powerful. Everything delicious in the cake can be also found in the fine nuances of this wine: bitter chocolate, nut aromas, hints of coffee, caramel and tobacco.

Gâteau au Chocolat and sweet wines: a carousel of tastes and sweet sin and definitely worth it.

Christina Fischer

Christina Fischer is ranked among the most renowned sommeliers in Germany. She is not only the owner of the prominent restaurant in Cologne called "Fischers Weingenuss & Tafelfreuden," but she also participates in various tasting juries and is an internationally recognized wine expert. Numerous interviews and television performances called TV Sommelière in VOX-Kochduell have made her famous across Germany. She tastes innumerable wines all year round and writes assessments of them. She has collaborated on many books concerning wine topics.

The wine expert and restaurateur acquired her extensive knowledge over the course of her various activities in Germany and abroad. Her hotel management education in the hotel Inter Continental Düsseldorf was followed by two years in the Inter Continental Hyde Park Corner in London. After returning to Cologne, she took over restaurant management in the "Soufflé" and worked simultaneously as a sommelier. The next rung on her career ladder was the post of sommelier in the three-star restaurant "Schiffchen" in Düsseldorf Kaiserswerth. Christina Fischer changed to the Cologne restaurant "Mäxwell" for two years, performing the same job and later she moved to the renowned hotel-restaurant "Brenner'scher Hof," also in Cologne.

In 1996, Christina Fischer opened her own restaurant "Fischers Weingenuss & Tafelfreuden" in Hohenstaufenring in Cologne. Finally, the wine-obsessed restaurateur could realize her dreams. According to Christina, the guest should be the center of attention. The very involved service and kitchen staff prepares fresh cross-cultural dishes and a numerous range of wines every day. There are more than 700 bottled wines and 40 wines are also offered in glasses. Many of the wines can be bought through the wine shop "Take away." The Catering Service of Fischers Weingenuss & Tafelfreuden is tailored to the respective event's needs. Moreover, a team of experts offers enjoyable wine seminars and events in the cozy wine cellars.

Christina Fischer was awarded "Förderpreis Pro Riesling" for her versatile activities in wine topics and gastronomy and a year later, she was also awarded the "Wine By the Glass Award" from the magazine *Decanter* and she won the "Moët Hennessy Team-Trophy" along with her restaurant staff. The professional jury selected Christina Fischer "Wirtin des Jahres 2000" (Winegrower of the Year 2000) and in the same year, her restaurant was awarded first price for "Beste Übersee-Weinkarte Deutschlands 2000" (Best Overseas Wine List of Germany 2000) by the magazine *Der Feinschmecker* and Robert Mondavi. A year later, Gault Millau Deutschland honored Christina Fischer as the "Sommelier of the year 2001."

Speaking the language of wine

When experts talk about wine, it often sounds very complex. At the same time, professional wine language usually uses everyday words and terms and is not as incomprehensible as it may appear at first. Would you like to describe the wine or simply explain its taste impressions? The following terms will help you to understand wine better.

ABBOCCATO:
Italian specification for half-dry wine.

ABOCADO:
Spanish specification for half-dry wine.

ACIDIFICATION:
Enrichment of the must by lemon and malic acid.

ACIDS:
Various acids such as tartaric acid or malic acid are indispensable to the quality of a wine and give it a refreshing strength.

ACRE:
2.5 acres are 1 hectare.

AFTERTASTE:
The short or long taste impression left on the palate by wine after swallowing. A long aftertaste signifies a top quality wine. A weak aftertaste is often a sign of an insufficient acid content.

AGE:
A positive or negative specification for wines, depending on whether wines are classified as "old" according to their vintage or taste.

AGRICOLA VITIVINICOLA:
Wine growing estate in Italy.

AIRING:
The wine is put into contact by careful pouring into a decanter (decanting) with air (oxygen).

ALCOHOL:
An important part. Content should not be too high. It is created through the fermentation of grape sugar in alcohol and carbon acid.

ALLIER-OAK:
French oak, which is used for making Barrique-casks with fine, porous wood.

AMPELOGRAPHY:
Science of the vine types.

ANNATA:
Italian word for vintage

ARDENT:
Strong red wines rich in alcohol with harmonious body.

AROMA:
The completeness of the substances granting the wine its smell and taste.

AROMATIC:
Wines from a very distinct vine usually have an aromatic bouquet.

ASSEMBLAGE:
Wines from different types of vine blended advantageously.

ASTRINGENT:
High and young acids can lead to dry effects in the mouth. This furry, dull feeling in the mouth results from immature tannin or concentrated tannin sharpness or wood casks.

AUSBRUCH:
In Austria, a specification for high quality, sweet Botrytis-wines.

AUTOCHTHONE TYPE OF VINE:
The type of vine, which is only grown in single regional vicinity.

BALANCE:
A wine with a harmonious taste.

BLANK:
Wines, of which aroma and smell do not develop are called blank

BARRIQUE:
French specification for a small, oak wood cask. Through the development in the Barrique, tannin is released from wood, which passes on to the wine. Originally, it was developed for Bordeaux wines. Today, development in the Barrique is practiced around the world.

BÂTONAGE:
Stirring yeast in the cask with a cane

BEERENAUSLESE (WINE MADE FROM SPECIALLY SELECTED GRAPES):
Wines from over-mature, sweet grapes. The fourth level in the hierarchy of wine quality.

BIOLOGICAL ACID DEGRADATION (BSA):
Biological acid degradation usually takes place after alcoholic fermentation. It describes all chemical procedures leading to the degradation of malic acid by microorganisms, which change into milder lactic acid by the breakdown of carbon acid.

BITE, BITING:
A strong impression which the wine leaves on the tongue. If it lacks bite, then the wine is shallow.

BITTER, BITTERNESS:
A taste nuance of the tannin substance which usually comes out with the wines from immature vintage. During the maturation of the wine, the initial bitterness often disappears.

BLANC DE BLANC:
Only pressed from white grapes sparkling wine or champagne from 100% Chardonnay-grapes.

BLANC DE NOIRS:
Wine with a bright color, gained from red grape, which come into contact only briefly, or not at all, with the must.

BÖCKSER (PUTRESCENT TASTE STENCH AND SMELL OF YOUNG WINES):
Fermentation mistake, which gives chiefly young wines an unpleasant stench of decayed eggs.

BODEGA:
Wine cellar or wine shop in Spain.

BODY:
Expression for heaviness, strength, and high extract con-

tent of a wine. However, wines with a gentle body can have finesse.

BOTTLE FERMENTATION:
Specification for German sparkling wines, grown according to the traditional Méthode champenoise.

Botrytis cinerea:
Mushroom which bursts the grape skins and draws water from the grapes. Indispensable for the production of top quality sweet wines.

BURNT:
Wines which have a high alcohol level and little fruit can smell burnt.

BRUT:
Term for dry champagne and sparkling wines.

BOUQUET:
The aroma of a wine perceived in the nose.

BUTTERY:
Rich, fatty taste, which chiefly comes out in wines matured in yeast and aged in the Barrique cask.

CAPSULE:
Protective cover for the cork.

CARBON ACID FERMENTATION:
Macération carbonique. The fermentation of the unground red grapes in an oxygen vacuum, which produces particularly succulent wines.

CASA:
Italian specification for a firm/company.

CASK SMELL:
Stale, unpleasant stench, resulting from old, inadequately treated casks.

CASK TASTE:
Musty, dull, woody taste

CAVA:
Official Spanish specification for sparkling wine produced according to Méthode champenoise.

CAVE:
French word for cellar.

CEDARWOOD:
A warm, soft smell, reminiscent a cigar box.

CHARACTER:
A wine possessing all positive characteristics of its vine type.

CHARMANT:
Expression for relatively irrelevant, trivial or light wines.

CHAPTILISING/SUGAR ENRICHMENT:
French word for enriching of the must with sugar before the fermentation, in order to achieve a higher alcohol content of the wine.

CHÂTEAU:
Often used term for a winegrowing estate in France. It can refer to a castle as well as to a small estate or property. No classification!

CHÈNE:
French word for oak.

CLARIFYING:
Wine-cultivation measure. By means of adding legally permitted substances, the undesirable parts are bound and excluded. Clarifying substances stay in the wine.

CLASSIFICATION:
Special highlighting of locations and wine growers. Common especially in Burgundy and Bordelais (Médoc, Saint-Emilion, Graves) for many years. In Germany – with the exception of the first wine in Rheingau – classifications have not had official and legal character.

CLASSICO:

Italian specification for the best locations within a DOC.

CLEAN:

A flawlessly, pure wine.

CLONE:

Variant of a specific type of vine.

CLOS:

French specification for a walled vineyard.

CLOSED:

Young or immature wines can be closed in smell and taste and usually open after some time in storage.

COLOR:

Significant in the assessment of wines. The color and the corresponding color reflections can be helpful when determining the type of vine, the origin and the age.

COLORING:

Coloring substances of the grapes are located in the skin and not in the juice. For a red wine to obtain its color, the pressed grapes have to stay for some time in the must. At that time, the juice absorbs the coloring from the burst skins. Rosé wines require a brief contact with the skins in order to obtain their slightly rose color.

COMMUNE:
French word for a municipality.

CONCORD:
All perceptible substances complement one another. Wines, rich in nuances, should possess this characteristic.

CONSTANCY:
The continuing perception of taste and aroma substances after swallowing. It is measured by its length. As a rule, a wine is better, the longer its full taste lingers in the mouth

CORK:
A stopper from oak cork, which contributes to the mature of the wine. Over the recent years, many problems have arisen with faulty corks, which have made these wines inconsumable. For simple wines, drunk within a shorter period, screw stoppers and artificial corks can be used.

CORKY:
Unpleasant musty stench and smell resulting in an invisible mold in the cork.

COSECHA:
Spanish word for harvest or vintage.

COZY:
Full-bodied, thick, soft and often very harmonious.

Crémant:
French specification for a sparkling wine produced outside of Champagne.

Cremig:
Specialist expression for sparkling wines which show carbon acid.

Crianza:
Specification for wines which mature in wood.

Crossbreed:
A blend of American and American types of vine.

Cru:
French term for a specific growth (location, vineyard). Important: has to do with above average quality. More specific specifications for it are Cru Classé, Cru Bourgeois or Premier Cru. Similar placements are exclusively limited to the areas of Bordelais and Burgundy in France, with various meanings for various regions.

Cru Bourgeois:
Bordeaux-wine below the quality level Cru Classé.

Cuvée:
A blend of two or more types of vine or types of wine to achieve an optimal result. It is usually done for trial in the cellar (Assemblage).

DECANTING:

Pouring wines from the bottle into a decanter. It is intended for the careful removing of grape substance or deposit created during the storing process. Wines are also decanted so that they come in contact with oxygen. By means of the procedure of oxidation, young or sharp tannin and tannin substances are reduced. Attention, old wines can quickly oxidize during this procedure!

DEMI-SEC:

French word for half-dry.

DEPOT:

It is formed by means of mature or long storing, chiefly in the case of red wines. The lees of solid parts can be coarse grained and also dusty. Depot is removed by careful decanting.

DEPTH:

The taste of such wine develops on the tongue in unexpected dimensions: thick, full-bodied and shows various layers or levels.

DOMAINE:

French word for a winegrowing estate.

DOSAGE:

Mixture of must, sugar (liquor) and wine given to wine and sparkling wine.

DOUX:
A French word for sweet.

DRY:
A taste impression of wines rich in tannin.

DRY:

Taste specification for the German wine with the rest sugar content of minimal 0.9 oz per quart in a specific relation to sharpness (according to the formula: sharpness plus 2). A wine with 0.24 oz of sharpness per quart can also contain 0.3 oz of sugar per quart, to be still classified as dry.

DRY WINE MADE FROM SPECIALLY SELECTED GRAPES:
In Austria and Germany, a specification for wine, which was pressed from dried, noble grapes.

DULL:
A watery, light, little smelling wine without aftertaste.

EARTHY:
A paraphrase for mineral marked wines, whose soil structure is reflected in the smell: for instance Muschelkalk, flint or also deep, rich clay soils.

EISWINES:
Highly concentrated wine from grapes, plucked and pressed in the frozen state (at least 19°F).

ELEGANT:
The proportions of the wine (aroma, taste, content and extract) are finely consonant and harmoniously balanced.

EMPTY:
Weak, blank. No perceptible taste.

ENOLOGY:
Science of wine.

ENOTECA:
An Italian word for wine shop.

ENRICHMENT:
Strictly stipulated in the German Wine Act of 1971: the addition of sugar is banned. Some exceptions are provided for putting sugar into QbA wines before fermentation so that these contain a higher content of alcohol.

EQUILIBRIUM:
The wine contains all desirable elements and has an ideal balance of smell, fruit, extract and alcohol.

EUCALYPTUS:
A description for specifying a spicy aroma, which resembles eucalyptus.

EXTRACT:
The sum of the aromatic wine elements without alcohol,

sharpness, sugar and water. The following belong to it: glycerin, tannin, and artificial coloring as well as minerals. The higher the extract is, the better the wine is. An average, good red wine has at least ½–1 oz of extract per quart. With top quality wines, it is more than 1 oz per quart.

FAINT:
Old, dull, and heavy without any finesse.

FATTORIA:
An Italian word for a wine growing estate in Toscana

FATTY:
Taste and consistency fill up the entire mouth. Fatty wines can be heavy and discordant.

FEATURELESS:
Instable balance of the wine due to low sharpness.

FERRIC:
Mineral taste impression, which results from the soil or terroir.

FERMENTATION:
Alcoholic fermentation is the conversion of sugar to alcohol and carbon dioxide. The fermentation is started by yeast, which exists naturally in the grape or is added as purely cultivated yeast to the must.

FINE:
Expression for balanced, harmonious quality.

FINESSE:
Flamboyant wines marked by permanence, consistence and other qualities. Taste and aroma are optimally integrated as well.

FIRM:
Taste variety, which affects the palate and tongue with a strong sharpness, tannin substances and a feeling of youth and power.

FLOWER, FLOWERY, FLORAL:
First degree of the bouquet. Positive taste impression: one refers to a noble, fine or gentle flower.

FRESH:
Youthful liveliness and ingenuity connected with sharpness.

FRIZZANTE:
Italian word for sparkling.

FULL:
A full-bodied, constant wine, which fills the palate with taste substances, which are tuned in a full-bodied manner.

FÙT DE CHÈNE:
A French word for an oak wood cask.

GENTLE:
A fine, filigreed wine with gentle fruit notes and subtle taste.

GLYCERIN:
Trivalent alcohol, which is formed in the course of the fermentation and leads to a sweet perception in the mouth. It grants the wine its full-bodied character and body. The richer in alcohol the wine, the higher the glycerin content. Glycerin leaves a "church window" on the glass.

GRAN RESERVA:
Spanish wine, which matures at least 24 months in the oak cask and then 36 months in the bottle.

GRAND CRU:
A specification for high quality wines from Burgundy and Bordelais. The meaning is, however, different: in Burgundy, Grand Cru is the highest level; in Bordelais, it only stands for a great wine and can be applied to high and also low qualities.

GRAPE SEPARATION:
The separation of grapes from the skins, also the skin-removed grapes or combs. Grape separation leads to fewer tannin substances in the must and in the late must.

GRASSY:

An immature, green, almost astringent taste, which results from heavy pressing or from grapes plucked early.

GREEN:

A wine, which tastes and smells grassy and immature.

HALF DRY:

Taste specification for German wines with the upper boundary of 0.65 oz. of rest sugar per quart. The sugar content must be in a specific relation to sharpness (according to the formula sharpness plus 10). This abstract term was introduced, since especially sharp wines from the northern wine growing areas with a relatively high content of rest sugar taste dry.

HARMONIOUS:

All content substances must smell and taste in a balanced relation.

HARD:

Wines when they have young tannin and strong sharpness.

HARVEST:

The harvest period is described as harvest or vintage. At the same time, the mature grade of the grapes determines the harvest time. The plucked grapes are denoted as vintage.

Heavy:
Full-bodied and rich in alcohol.

Hectare:
1 hectare is 2.5 acres.

Herblike:
Smell notes in the bouquet; also described as grassy.

Hollow:
A wine with little character and no expression.

Honest:
A good, simple wine.

Imbottigliato nell origine:
Italian word for filling by the producer.

Immature:
Wines produced from an immature vintage. Wines which have not achieved maturity, but still have development potential.

Impériale:
Large bottles with 1.5 gallons of filling quantity.

Infiltrated:
Unfiltered wine which contains fine, subtle aromas.

INSIPID:
Bland, lacking sharpness.

KABINETT (HIGH QUALITY GERMAN WHITE WINE):
Since the introduction of the German Wine Act in 1971, it has been the lowest level for German quality wines. The minimum must weight is according to the cultivated area from 67 to 82 grades Oechsle.

KEEN:
An unharmonious composition of particular components. Sharpness is synonymous with keen when slightly subdued.

LATE HARVEST:
An English word for late vintage

LATE VINTAGE:
The second level of the German quality scale. It comes after Kabinett and before selection

LENGTH, LONG:
Wines which leave a lasting sensation in the mouth.

LIVELY:
A fresh, zesty wine with stirring sharpness.

LIGHT:
Relatively little alcohol and body. A weak bouquet.

LOCATION:
Area in which the vine is grown.

LUSCIOUS:
A simple, tasty wine of good, but not best quality.

LUSTER:
High extract and alcohol content. A mark of wines from mature grapes.

MAGNUM:
Bottle size with the content of 1½ quarts.

MALOLACTIC FERMENTATION:
The so-called second fermentation, in which malic acid is converted by a specific bacteria into softer lactic acid.

MARC:
A French word for marc. Chiefly, also a specification for marc.

MARC:
Specification for pressing squeezed-out rests as well as for firing resulting from the distillation. Marc or marc brand correspond to Italian Grappa and French Marc.

MASSIVE:
A full-bodied, heavy, sometimes robust wine.

MASTER OF WINE:
Title, awarding of which is preceded by extensive tests and exams.

MATURE:
A mature wine at its peak taste.

MAZERATIONS-PROCEDURE:
Carbon acid fermentation

MEDICINE TONE:
A perceptible smell resembling medicine and the drugstore. No negative criterion.

MELLOW:
Harmonious, well-balanced, full-bodied and well-proportioned wine.

METALLIC:
Bad tone with an unpleasant smell of iron.

MILD:
lovely

MILLÉSIME:
French word for vintage.

MINERAL:
Wines grown in the mineral soil which reproduce these terroir components in bouquet and smell.

MIS EN BOUTEILLE AU CHÂTEAU/DOMAINE:
French word for filling by the producer.

MIXED SET:
Wines simultaneously gained from multiple vine types.

MOUSSE:
Bubbles in champagne and sparkling wine.

MUST:
Ground and crushed grapes which still contain the complete juice.

MUST:
Pressed juice from grapes intended for further processing.

MUST WEIGHT:
Measurement of how many ounces one quart of must at 68°F is heavier than one quart of water. The must weight is measured in Germany in Oechsle-grade: one quart of must, which weighs 2.2 lbs, has 70 Oechsle grades.

MUST FERMENTATION:
Cleaning the must prior to the fermentation.

NERVOUS:
Succulent wine with good, integrated, strong sharpness.

NEUTRAL:
The wine has no perceptible fragrance or taste.

OAK SMELL:
It usually comes from storage in Barrique casks. Possible aromas are: toasted wood, vanilla, cedar, freshly cut oak wood, smoked and slightly burnt touches and ash.

OECHSLE-GRADE:
Measurement scale for sugar content based on th specific weight of grape juice. The maturity of the grape can then be specified.

OFFICIAL CONTROL NUMBER (AP):
According to the German Wine Act, it is a certification stipulating that wine can be put into circulation as quality wine. The AP must be placed on the label.

OILY:
A viscous, creamy wine, which leaves an oily feeling in the mouth. The term is chiefly used for top sweet wines.

ORGANOLEPTIC:
Sense perceptions and acuities during the wine tasting e.g. color, smell and taste.

OXIDATION/OXIDIZED:

Opposite of reductive. The air affect on the wine. With young wines it is desirable, since they open earlier in contact with oxygen. With older wines, oxidation can quickly go the other way and the wines acidify. Wines which already oxidigized in the cask or in the bottle, are bad.

OXIDATIVE:

Defect in the wine, which contains many aldehydes because of long oxygen contact, and is therefore poor quality.

PEPPY:

A specification for heavy, over-sweet or obtrusive aromatized wines.

PHYLLOXERA:

Disease brought from America.

PIQUANT:

Wines which taste fresh and succulent with stimulating sharpness and bite.

PLAIN:

A simple wine without height or depth.

PLEASANT:

Nice wine without height and depth, but not very demanding.

PLENTEOUS:

Wine, not unconditionally sweet, with a feeling of opulent profusion.

POOR:

A weak, empty wine without body.

PRELIMINARY MUST:

High value part of the must, which, following the grinding of grapes, flows out directly after the pressing procedure without any pressing.

PREMATURE:

Wine which has developed too quickly.

PRESSING:

Old wine pressing from wood, mostly replaced by pneumatically operated pressing machines. During the pressing process, grapes or the must are pressed out for gaining the must.

PRIMEUR:

New wine, for instance Beaujolais Primeur.

PRODUCER'S FILLING:

Wine which exclusively originates from one's own grapes.

PURE SORT:

Wine produced from a single type of vine.

PURE TINGE:
Wines which appear clear and fine both in the bouquet and taste.

QUALITY WINE (QBA):
Quality wine from specific wine growing areas. According to the German Wine Act, it deals with the preliminary stage of special quality wines.

QUINTA:
A Portuguese word for wine growing estate.

RACKING:
A cellar-technical procedure for pouring the wine from the casks/vessel into another, clean container. Simultaneously, the separation of the clear wine from the remaining grounds parts, for instance yeast.

RÉCOLTE:
French word for harvest.

REDUCTIVE:
Tasty and strong wine grown in an oxygen vacuum.

REFRESHING:
A specification for lively, light, sparkling wine which often contains invisible carbon acids.

REMOVING THE GROUNDS AND CLEANING THE NECK OF THE BOTTLE FROM YEAST:
Removing the grounds formed in the course of the second fermentation of champagne in the bottle.

RESERVA:
Quality term for Spanish wines, matured for some time in the cask.

RÉSERVE:
A French term without any wine relevant meaning.

REST SWEETNESS/REST SUGAR:
The existent sugar content in the finished wines. It can be either a natural remaining stock of the fermentation, or added grape juice (sweet reserve).

RICH IN ALCOHOL:
The specification for wines with have a high content of alcohol. Rich in alcohol wines often smell burnt and unusually heavy.

ROBUST:
A strong, abundant, really substantial wine.

ROUGH:
Neither the taste nor consistencies of such wine are pleasant. They often leave a prickly, astringent or sour taste.

SCHILFWEIN:
Austrian specialty wine, whose grapes are dried for a longer period of time in straw.

SEC/SECCO/SECO:
French/Italian/Spanish term for dry.

SECOND FERMENTATION:
malolactic fermentation.

SECT:
Sparkling wine, produced in Germany, in which the basic wines originate from various European countries.

SÉLECTION DE GRAINS NOBLES:
A term used in Alsace for wines made from specially selected grapes.

SHARP:
Unharmonious wine with taste substances such as tannin.

SHORT:
The wine has no "tail," or aftertaste.

SLENDER:
Wine in which extract substances are well-developed, without being excessive compared with other components.

SMELL, DAINTY:
A fine, gentle smell.

SMOKY:
These taste components can usually be found in wines aged in the Barrique.

SOMMELIER:
French word for wine cellar.

SORT:
The character of a wine, the big picture.

SORT TYPICAL:
Aroma typification, which results from the type of vine.

SPARKLING WINE:
Slightly sparkling wine.

SPARKLING WINE:
Generic term for wines with a carbon acid impression of at least 3 bars.

SPARSE:
The wine lacks extracts, body, alcohol and taste substances. No synonym for light.

SPICY:
Wine with spicy aromas from types of vine such as Gewürztraminer, Cabernet Sauvignon or Syrah

SPIRITUOUS:
Wines, in which alcohol comes out unpleasantly.

SPUMANTE:
An Italian word for sparkling wine.

STALE:
Flat wines.

STEELY:
White wine with distinct sharpness.

STILL WINE:
Wine without carbon acids.

STRONG:
Wines which are rich in alcohol, extracts and smell.

SUBSTANTIAL:
The opposite is true for this word suggesting elegance, combined with an overloaded aroma and a strong alcohol taste.

SUCCULENT:
A succulent wine is tough, fatty, succulent and oily, but it is not strong.

SUCCULENT:
A full-bodied wine which tempts you to drink more.

SUCCULENT:
Describes both the bouquet and the taste. It illustrates the richness of a wine gained from healthy and mature grapes and the typical fruit character accompanied with it. Succulence is usually accompanied by a residual touch of sugar.

SUPPLE:
A quality, high value, smooth, mellow and pleasant wine with balanced sharpness.

SUR LIE:
French word for wines stored in yeast. White wines obtain a refreshing and succulent aroma.

SWEET:
The specification for wines with higher sugar content than half dry wines. It can, but does not have to be, placed on the label. Mild wines with harmonic sweetness and balanced content in bouquet and taste substances.

SWEET RESERVE:
Unfermented grape juice used for sweetening wines.

TABLE WINE:
The lowest grade of German wines without reference to origin.

TANNIN SUBSTANCE:

The tannin substance – also described as tannin – exists in the skins, seeds and stems of the grapes. Various types of vines also have different tannin contents. With high tannin content, which is demonstrated by young wines or wines from immature grapes, the mucous membrane usually constricts (astringent). With red wines, tannin decomposes its aggressive effects and changes into a mature, soft form, which supports the taste of the wine and grants it its durability. An additional tannin substance is created in the wine during storage in wood casks, especially in Barrique casks.

TANNIN:

Also described as tannin substance, it is chiefly found in red wines. Tannin can produce an astringent feeling in the mouth, and it feels furry and dry on the palate. Tannin like other content substances, decomposes during storage. The wine thus becomes full-bodied and can be stored longer.

TEMPERATURE CONTROL:

Measurement of the must temperature in the course of fermentation, used for controlling the fermentation duration and fermentation procedure.

TENUTA:

Italian word for wine growing estate or vineyard.

TERROIR:

French word for soil and harmony with nature.

THICK:

A wine with compact body.

THOROUGHLY FERMENTED:

Wines in which the sugar changes into alcohol during fermentation, and which do not contain any noteworthy rests of sugar. At the same time, with their high acid content, thoroughly fermented wines smell heavy and cutting.

TOAST:

Toast taste is found in various intensities in wines matured in the Barrique.

TOUGH:

The wine is tough when particular elements fail to harmonize

UNHARMONIOUS

The particular content substances of a wine are discordant. Especially prominent in young wines requiring storage.

VANILLA:

Smell usually found in wines aged in new Barrique casks.

VARIANT:
Distinct, lively wine, in which sharpness markedly comes out, but not unpleasantly.

VENDANGE TARDIVE:
French word for late vintage. It is qualitatively higher than the German late vintage.

VEGETABLE:
Wine with green, vegetable and/or vegetative aromas

VELVET:
A term usually used for red wines that leave a soft taste behind due to their pleasantly mature, well-integrated tannin substances and fruity sweetness.

VIGNOBLE:
A French word for vineyard.

VIN DE PAYS:
A simple *vin ordinaire* with the specifications of the determined geographic origin.

VIN DE TABLE:
French table wine without the specifications of the origin.

VINEGAR TONE:
Indication of imperfect wines, which smell intensely of vinegar extract.

Vinification:
French word for wine preparation

Vintage:
The third German quality level for wines from mature, top quality sweet grapes

Well-seasoned taste:
Taste notes of an old wine which has taken on heavy storage bouquet (oxidation bouquet). With top quality wines, the so-called noble, well-seasoned taste can also show enrichment.

Vintage champagne:
Champagne from wines of a vintage.

Watery:
A weak wine with a watery taste.

Wide, round bottle:
Traditional, wide, round bottle form, used chiefly in Franconia.

Wine growing:
Also vinification or vinyfying. The specialist term for the development of a wine in the cellar from the fermentation to filling.

WINE STONE:

Harmless potassium cyanide in the form of crystals, formed due to alcohol formation and cooling down after the fermentation. Most people do not find it obtrusive.

YEAST:

Unicellular, vegetal microorganisms capable of converting sugar into alcohol. Wine yeast consists mostly of saccharomyces cerevisiae.

YEAST TONE, YEASTY:

Yeast can be smelled in young wines or when they mature in the yeast.

YIELD:

An important factor in the quality of a wine. The principle is as follows: the less the yield quantity, the higher the extract values of the grapes. The yield can be regulated by the winegrower by means of the corresponding first cut of the vine as well as by pruning of the blossom and immature grapes.

YOUNG WINE:

Wine before filtration, which lies in the yeast or contains rest quantities of yeast.

ABBREVIATIONS:

AC/AOC:

Appellation Contrôlée / Appellation d Origine Contrôlée. An officially stipulated specification by the French Government for state-controlled wines. The control comprises and guarantees a specific cultivated area, production methods, used types of vine and yield quantities.

AP:

Official control number. A reference stating that a German wine may be put into circulation as quality wine. Compulsory specifications on German labels.

BSA:

Biological acid degradation. It usually takes place after the alcoholic fermentation. It describes all chemical procedures, which lead to the fall of malic acid by means of microorganisms which convert into milder lactic acid under the breakdown of carbon acid.

DLG:

German Agricultural Organization. It grants nationwide awards and gives wine seals.

DO:

Denominación de Origen is the Spanish specification for the controlled origin of the wine.

DOC:

Denominazione di Origine Controllata. Since 1964, the Italian specification of origin with regulations concerning the cultivated area borders, types of vine and wine growing.

DOCA:

Denominación de Origen Calificada. Qualified Spanish wines, Rioja wines were awarded for the first time in 1991.

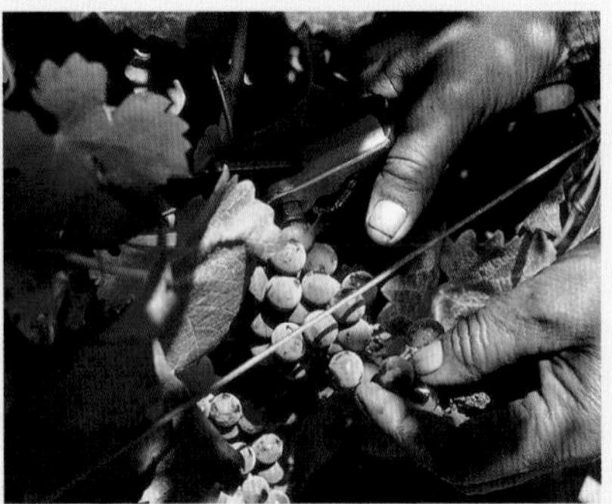

DOCG:

Denominazione di Origine Controllata e Garantita. The highest level of the Italian Wine Act, containing mainly stricter quantity limits as the DOC.

DWI:

German Wine Institute

IGT:

Indicazione Geografica Tipica. A specification which was introduced for Italian regional wines in 1997. The demands for the alcohol content and quantity limits are below the DOC level.

INAO:

Institut National des Appellations d'Origine. The French body supervising the permission of the AOC wines.

VdlT:

Vino de la Tierra. Spanish vin ordinaire from a specific cultivated area, which has no DO-status.

VdM:

Vino de Mesa. Spanish table wine, whose grapes originate from several vicinities.

VDP:

Union of the German Quality Wine Growing Estates (Vereinigung der deutschen Prädikatsweingüter). A voluntarily union of quality oriented wine growing estates with determined specifications for wine growing.

VdT:

Vino da Tavola. Italian table wine with the lowest demands. On the label, only the color, alcohol content and country of origin can be stated.

THANKS TO...

The most important point: cooperation! This book, along with all wine knowledge, would not be possible without "winy spirit." Bring all your enthusiasm, character, personality and knowledge every time you try a new wine. Our competent author who has been bitten by the wine bug – Ingo Swoboda (photo) – worked tirelessly on the text and content. The entire kitchen and service team of Fischer offered the basis and support for all wine-related activities. Astrid Müllers, manager of Sommelier Consult, deals with wine every day and supported us considerably with pictures and topic choice. We owe the splendid photos to the creative team of Armin Faber and Thomas Pothmann. Christine Balais, Jan Bimboes, Götz Drewitz, Christian Frens, Katja Giessler, Petra Mohr and many others are responsible for organizing seminars and propagating wine knowledge. Thanks a million for your boundless and inspiring enthusiasm!

Christina Fischer, April 2003